SOWING THE GOSPEL IN JAPANESE SOIL

Understanding Japanese Religious Beliefs

John Wm. Mehn

Gospel Rest Resources

Sowing the Gospel in Japanese Soil: Understanding Japanese Religious Beliefs
© *2019 by John Wm. Mehn. Version 1.5.2.*
All rights reserved
Gospel Rest Resources 2019
Published by Gospel Rest Resources: 602 John St. Pecatonica, IL 60163
www.GospelRest.com

ISBN 9781706566441

English transliterations of Japanese words and phrases use the modified Hepburn system unless the original source indicates otherwise. Macrons have been used in this book to signify long vowels in Japanese, except in cases where the word is well-known such as Osaka, Tokyo, Shinto, etc. Japanese personal names are listed in Western order.

Some illustrations by Sarah Roberts.
Cover Photo by Yasunai Nakamura
First Printing 2019.

Table of Contents

Introduction

Sowing the Gospel in Japanese Soil

> The Lord has assigned to each his task. I planted the seed, Apollos watered it, but God has been making it grow. So neither the one who plants nor the one who waters is anything, but only God, who makes things grow. The one who plants and the one who waters have one purpose (1 Cor 3:5-8).

I had gotten to know soil pretty well. I had planted many trees, shrubs, and crawled around on my knees laying sod. For several years, I was a professional landscaper, and soil was a big part of my job. I dug it, I moved it, I loaded it, and I planted flowers, groundcover, and evergreens in it. I went home often with my clothes covered with soil and soil stuck to my skin.

As a missionary in Japan, I have tried to perceive of the cultural roots of the Japanese, above all their religious beliefs. As an American I was transplanted into Japan and I strove to flourish in Japanese soil. I have endeavored to adapt, adjust, relate, and enjoy living and ministering in this soil. Most of the time I feel that I have made progress, but still I often I feel have so much to go. I continue in disbelief even when Japanese might tell me that I think, act, or speak like a Japanese.

To make ministry in Japan effective, I have talked to many Japanese, read several books, and discussed at length with both missionaries and Japanese leaders. Often, as we discussed we had more questions than answers, and there never seemed any quick answers. We were told time and again that someone had found "the key to reaching Japan" but they never seemed to unlock Japan and we felt the situation was never that simple.

We kept coming back to the same basic question, sometimes described with different words: How do we sow the gospel in Japanese soil so that it thrives with multiplying disciples and healthy churches?

I was very familiar with the soil of where I grew up. Illinois USA is one of the most fertile places on our planet. I was even used to the smell of the soil, especially after a summer's rain. I felt unaccustomed to the soil of Japan and Japan seemed very unfamiliar. The learning process was exciting but sometimes felt like being on a moving treadmill that did not seem to make any forward progress. Maybe you are like me, I enthusiastically continued learning about the culture, but so many more questions kept coming. This experience made it feel like the longer I was in Japan the less familiar I was with the culture.

To be effective in sowing the gospel we must know our seed and the soil. I had been sharing in seminars these ideas about culture and Japan for some time. From those experiences, equipping people to share the gospel with Japanese, I realized they needed somewhat more than an occasional seminar. This was a needy area no matter if workers were part of the new wave of people sent to Japan or whether they had long experience struggling with the missiological enigma of Japan. As I shared the possibilities of this book with many people, I was very encouraged as they showed great interest in reading what I planned to write. I saw an opportunity in writing this book to equip many to sow the gospel with the Japanese.

I am in a long line of people who have written on the gospel and the culture of Japan. I have tried to present a broadminded evangelical perspective on some complex issues. The presentation is not meant to be academic, but it does touch on many academic concepts. The purpose is to put comprehensive understanding into practical ministry. I do not think I present any radical or novel approaches, but maybe you will choose to disagree with me. I hope this book will generate more dialogue and discussion on these issues.

This book has several limitations. It is not meant to be exhaustive, but just a short introduction touching on a several points of a huge topic. Here I do not have all the answers as I really have more questions. In this book, my purpose is that by interacting with some key Japanese concepts, Christian theology, and missiology you will be better equipped to present more relevant witness that will transform Japan's worldview and society.

How do we understand the religious beliefs of the Japanese people and how do we sow the seed of the gospel in such a way that it germinates, grows, and thrives in the soil of Japan? The soil of Japan is its culture. Soil consists of many components and likewise so does culture. This is a book about soil, culture, and Japan. To begin our study of "soil science" we need to overview some basics of culture.

Lloyd Kwast has a very helpful diagram (figure one) explaining culture based on successive layers or depth of culture (Kwast 1992)[1].

---

[1]Lloyd Kwast himself admits that this diagram is

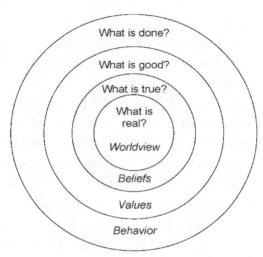

Figure 1 From Kwast 1992 "Understanding Culture"

The first level is behavior or what activities are being done. In Japan bowing, taking baths (*furo*), and removing shoes are a few Japanese examples of behaviors or practices. The second level is the level of values or what is good, or beneficial, or best. Values are the culture's operating system that encodes default decisions. Values are what should be done. Harmony, group orientation, hierarchy, cleanliness, and reserve (*enryō*) are just several Japanese cultural values.

Culture is like an iceberg in that much of it is underwater or invisible. Culture's influence on individuals is often imperceivable and people

---

incredibly simple and does not explain the complexities of culture. But for our purpose it can be a helpful starting point.

9

habitually adhere to cultural norms unconsciously. Behavior and values are often visible parts of the culture. We want to probe more deeply into these invisible zones of the Japanese culture.

The third level of culture is beliefs or what is true. These are operating beliefs that impact values and behavior. A majority of beliefs are religious in nature, which we will explore in Part One of this book. The fourth level of culture is worldview which answers the question what is real? As worldview influences every zone of the culture, it is far more important than any of the other levels. Worldview is like the atomic nucleus of the culture binding everything together. Our ultimate goal is to transform the cultural worldview and thus beliefs, values, and behavior will follow in turn.

In this book we will touch only lightly on certain religious practices and comment briefly on some Japanese cultural values (chapter six). The goal is to probe deeper and present a system of religious beliefs of the Japanese. These beliefs are from the culture's core or the worldview of the people.

This book is written in two parts, the first explores the soil of Japan and the second focuses on sowing the gospel in Japan. Each chapter will attempt to answer several key questions of our quest to penetrate the beliefs and worldview of the Japanese.

Part One: Will focus on the Japanese Soil, the beliefs and worldview that make up the Japanese culture.

Chapter One: The Nature of Religion in Japan. What is the underlying nature of Japanese beliefs? How do Japanese go about expressing their beliefs?

Chapter Two: Toward Understanding Japanese Worldview. What are some important issues when viewing the Japanese Worldview?

Chapter Three: A Model for Understanding Japanese Beliefs. How can we view Japanese beliefs together in a holistic framework?

Chapter Four: Understanding Japanese Religious Beliefs. What are common examples of popular religious beliefs and practices?

Chapter Five: The Five Japanese Belief Systems. What are the influences of each of the five Japanese belief systems? What about the Japanese and secularism?

Chapter Six: Japanese Religious Practices and Motivations. What are some of the Japanese religious practices? What are the motivations for following Japanese religious practices?

Part Two: Will focus on sowing the gospel in Japan, that the seed of the gospel germinates, grows, and thrives.

Chapter Seven: Understanding Contextualization. How do we adapt our mission approaches to produce a dynamic indigenous faith?

Chapter Eight: Towards Christian Advance in Japan. What are some issues of missiology and theology that may affect the advance of the gospel in Japan?

Chapter Nine: Sowing and Harvesting Practices. What are some ministry principles for sowing the gospel and preparing for the harvest?

Chapter Ten: Supernatural Faith. What is our supernatural Christian faith? Do we believe in our supernatural faith?

After first introducing the subject of culture we quickly considered the invisible parts of culture such as beliefs and worldview. To understand Japanese religious beliefs, we begin our investigation of Japanese soil with a look into the nature of religion in Japan.

Part One

The Japanese Soil

1

The Nature of Religion in Japan

How do Japanese perceive religious beliefs? In the introduction we have discussed briefly the nature of culture and the importance of worldview and beliefs. The Japanese culture and especially their religious worldview and beliefs have presented formidable challenges of presenting the gospel in the Japanese soil. To improve our understanding of Japanese religious beliefs we must know the underlying nature of religion in Japan. How do Japanese go about expressing and framing their beliefs?

Scene One
A group of women gather for a time of comfort through a craft and teatime with some Christians in Ishinomaki, Miyagi Prefecture, a city most effected by the triple disaster of earthquake, tsunami, and nuclear accident in 2011. These

15

women are from an area that experienced over 400 deaths in their immediate community. The discussion turns to their fear of using certain roads at night due to concern for ghosts (*yūrei*) in the area.

Scene Two

A long-term Japanese friend visits your home for dinner. In the genkan he takes out a case containing Buddhist prayer beads and fastens them to his wrist. He points to them to warn you not to try to convert him to Christianity.

Just what exactly is going on here? If these scenes are typical of Japanese religious beliefs, then how do we bring the gospel of Jesus Christ to the Japanese context. How do we sow the gospel in Japanese soil?

Japanese Soil

Religious surveys declare the majority of Japanese identify themselves with both Shintoism and Buddhism. However, religion in Japan "is a variegated tapestry created by the interweaving of at least five major strands: Shinto, Buddhism, Daoism, Confucianism and folk religion" (Earhart 2014, 2). As Japanese continue to move away from organized religion, they resist secularization and statistically demonstrate to be a spiritual people (Lewis 2018, 28-29) as evident from their religious behavior. "The Japanese identification with gods in nature, the importance of the family, the significance of specific rituals and amulets, the prominence of individual cults-these all integrate religious activities into everyday life" (Earhart 2014, 15).

When we understand the Japanese soil better, we can better communicate the gospel in sowing, watering, cultivating, and weeding. To share the gospel, meet heartfelt needs, and answer the longing of a people, we need to look not just at their behavior but deeper to their values, beliefs, and worldview. We desire to penetrate their worldview leading to truly indigenous belief in Christ. Communicating the gospel will be more effective if we progress from a framework that understands their religious belief system. This missiological challenge is also related to the difficulties of establishing Christian churches in Japanese soil (see Mehn 2017).

Everyday Japanese are increasingly less interested in organized religion but are extremely spiritual people, seeking meaning and fulfillment in the practical outcomes of folk religious practices (Macfarlane 2007, 175-77; cf. Netland 2015, 68). In Japanese folk religion the "various features of these religious and semi-religious systems were blended to meet the spiritual needs of the common people, who had to find religious meaning in the midst of their workaday life" (Hori 1968, xi).

Religion in Japan is Unstructured

Much of Japanese religion is a mix of formal religious concepts and animistic beliefs. Japanese most often follow the traditions of the local neighborhood shrines, rites and oral traditions of their immediate family or geographical area (Hiebert & Meneses 1995, 216). Attention is often placed with immanent beings of this world especially their local guardian deities.

In many ways' religion in Japan in the traditional sense resists any definition or systematic analysis. Some have tried to break down and analyze all the elements of Japanese religion. Dissecting may make things simpler but "the artificial separation of these traditions not only distorts the individual elements but also prevents ... gaining a total picture of Japanese religion" (Earhart 1969, 1). In Japan these religious beliefs, as Berentsen describes are "vaguely defined and diverse practices of local folk religion" (1985, 262). Asking Japanese to explain the origins of their beliefs is often fruitless as they often honestly respond they do not know. Unless they have been to a recent funeral, many cannot even tell you the major Buddhist school of their family temple. The Japanese do not have neat and tidy books of systematic theology. If we interviewed these women from Ishinomaki they would no doubt present us with several different solutions to these "wandering spirits."

For the Japanese the "logic" of their religion is that it meets their needs and that it is effective rather than it appears unified and rational. "The lack of rational logic in the religious field and the part which sentiment plays in the religiousness of the Japanese are in themselves deserving of a separate study... it seems almost impossible to present them in a synthesis of religious thought and doctrines... for most Japanese this problem seems senseless. They are not concerned about the ontological problems of their religions; what is important is religion as a practice, a cult" (Basabe 1972, 5-6).

Religion in Japan is unstructured and defies analysis because it borrows heavily from other religions and combines values that are contrary to common logic. "There can be no conflict between religions. Eclecticism is no problem. The relative has become absolute; the absolute has become relative" (Corwin 1972, 158-59). While Christianity has been accused of being "too logical," for the Japanese, the "logic" of their religion though unstructured is that it effectively works.

Religion in Japan is Adaptive

Many Japanese will be married in a Shinto ceremony and then have their funeral at a

Buddhist ceremony. This commonplace mixing and borrowing from other religious traditions means that Japanese folk religion "developed as an integral whole out of the interaction of many separate elements" (Hori 1968, 30). Folk religious practices all over Japan often follow a common stream of practices based on universal Japanese elements. However, in actuality most practices are adapted locally and vary considerably (Kodansha 1993, 387).

As Christian believers we want to understand the context of Japan and while holding to a high view of Scripture we adapt the forms, content, and practice of Christians beliefs in the Japanese setting. Because of this adaptive nature of Japanese religion there is a constant danger of syncretism or the compromise of gospel truth. One clear example of syncretism is the *Kakure Kirishitan* (hidden Christians) after the Tokugawa period who intermixed Buddhism, Mariolatry and Japanese folk religion. We need to practice critical contextualization that exegetes both the scriptures and the context as "good contextualization draws on scripture as its primary source but recognizes the significant role that context will play in shaping theology and practice" (Ott & Strauss 2010, 283–84). This process is to be conducted through the Christian community making the gospel more understandable while avoiding any compromise.

Story Three
Once I overheard two Christian believers from a prominent church discussing in detail their shared Chinese zodiac sign and horoscope as key influencers of their behavior and life direction. I did not hear their integration of a Christian Worldview and values.

We must provide deep answers for Japanese Christians while avoiding any compromise otherwise Japanese believers in Christ will profess faith but still hold on to previous religious beliefs. They will either move to syncretism and take both Christianity and Japanese religion and admix them or move to a practice what is called "split-level Christianity" where people hold two incompatible allegiances to a worldview or belief system.

Religion in Japan is Pragmatic

Folk beliefs attempt to answer many questions of life, the meaning in this life and the problem of death, well-being in this life and the problem of misfortunes, knowledge to decide and the problem of the unknown, and righteousness and justice and the problem of evil and injustice (Hiebert et al 1999, 74ff).

For the Japanese religion has the role of serving in difficult times. The old phrase *kurushii toki no kamidanomi* (turning to a god in time of trouble) is nearly synonymous with a definition of Japanese religion. For the Japanese, "religion is a means to secure material benefits. Numinous powers are called forth from the locale of the shrines to assist man in his walk through life" (Corwin 1972, 159).

As Japanese religion is so pragmatic, Reader and Tanabe have entitled their book: *Practically Religious, Worldly Benefits and the Common Religion of Japan.* Their thesis is that *genze riyaku*, which means "this-worldly benefits" or "practical benefits in this lifetime" is the central element to Japanese religion. The practical benefits of religion are "primarily material or physical gains such as good health, healing, success, or ... personal advancement in one's life path, ... personal well-being and freedom from problems" (Reader & Tanabe 1998, 2). This aspect of the practical benefits of religion is an important explanation of other aspects of Japanese society and culture. This pragmatic value is especially true for the youth of Japan as they use religion for immediate concrete problems (Swyngedouw 1993, 52). Japanese religious rituals are practically oriented. Japanese regularly practice rites and festivals, deal with purification and pollution, and seek good fortune.

Davis outlines the possible "specific, goal-oriented, ad hoc activities in search of this-worldly benefits" of a typical woman as she seeks marriage, bears a child, secure safety for her car, and blessing as their child prepares for school entrance examinations (Davis 1992, 24).

The beliefs about ghosts from those women from Ishinomaki lead to some very practical concerns. People who have died "bad deaths" become *muenbotoke* or nameless unknown spirits (Lewis 2013, 1). If these do not have proper rites performed on their behalf, they could become vengeful spirits (*goryō*) and take out vengeance on the living with cursing and misfortune.

We who are involved in sharing the gospel with Japanese must not neglect the "this worldly" benefits of belief in Christ, not merely share the promise of eternal life in heaven after death. We must also be aware of the danger of erring in the other direction, like in prosperity gospel theology, promising an easy life without suffering. In sowing the gospel with Japanese, we should challenge ourselves why the Christian religion in Japan is often viewed as impractical but instead intellectual and stiff.

Religion in Japan Centers on Ancestor Practices

The most commonly practiced aspect of Japanese religion is the worship and veneration of ancestors. These popular practices are conducted at home in front of the *butsudan* (Buddhist altar) or the *kamidana* (Shinto god shelf), in shrines and temples, at gravesites, and even at schools and in the workplace.

These religious beliefs and practices are not only a part of their religion but also the very center of their religion. "Ordinary people accept ancestor worship as something beyond any particular religion or something encompassing all religions... substantially it is their religion" (Chizuo 1985, 250). The belief and practices of ancestor worship have been described as the glue that binds the Japanese to each other and to previous generations. So it is very understandable that a son who had recently seen the death of his mother would wear prayer beads to continue his relationship with his mother after death. Religion in Japan emphasizes ancestor worship because it shares this worldview concerning man, death, spirits, and deities. "Japanese ancestor practices express the content of the reality of the Japanese worldview" (Ronan 1999, 4). This worldview is the core of Japanese folk religion and originates and perpetuates itself throughout generations through the ancestor cult (see chapter five).

Most Japanese live their religious lives with its corresponding beliefs and practices at the folk religion level. Their understanding of their religion is often unstructured, defies analysis, adapts by making use of many elements, and is intensely practical. The Japanese consider these religious values as "the intuitive, the useful, the inner experience, the conviviality of the group" and the concrete (Basabe 1972, 6).

Understanding this religious context is difficult and makes sowing the seed of the Christian gospel in the Japanese context extremely challenging. To facilitate evangelism and the growth of the church, in the next chapter, we now turn to a model for understanding Japanese religious beliefs. This model may assist us in grasping many Japanese beliefs in a more wholistic framework.

2

Toward Understanding Japanese Worldview

In the previous chapter to help us understand the soil of Japan we outlined the nature of Japanese religious beliefs. This chapter focuses on the worldview of the Japanese and how often we have blinders to what they perceive as reality.

Miyazaki's World
Throughout the world cultural elements from Japan have great influence such as design, architecture, fine art, fashion, and landscape gardening. A major influence has been Japanese pop culture including *manga* (graphic novels) and most especially film animation or *anime*.

For *anime* no one person is more quintessentially Japanese than the award-winning director Hayao Miyazaki. As Miyazaki is very concerned with Japanese cultural values and beliefs, his films have opened many minds to better enter the culture of Japan. Through his

Studio Ghibli and a partnership with Disney more of these Japanese *anime* films are being seen throughout the world.

Several of his films are based on stories from Western literature or include predominantly Western themes. However three of his films delve into the world of Japanese religious beliefs especially folk Shintoism and Buddhism. He uses these motifs to relate to characters or send a message like pacifism or environmentalism.

In Miyazaki's world everything including nature, trees, and water have a kind of living essence. Shinto's *yaorozunokami* or 8 million (or innumerable) gods or *kami* are imagined as elemental, powerful and dangerous beings that are sources of life and death. In these films, human characters interact with spirit characters, we are introduced to sacred sites or areas including Shinto shrines, and we view numerous fundamental Shinto symbols like *torii* (archway).

Miyazaki's 1997 *Princess Mononoke (Mononoke Hime)* shows the essence of the real world, a world of spirits where there is a war between spirits of the forest and human beings who are consuming the forest of natural resources. No film is more revealing of the unseen world of spirits than Miyazaki's most popular and Oscar winning 2001 *Spirited Away (Sen to Chihiro no Kami Kakushi)* that is filled with stories of ghosts and goblins and the struggle for purification.

One of his most endearing films is *My Neighbor Totoro* (*Tonari no Totoro*). So many children have seen this wonderful film of adventure and friendship as seen through two girls who recently moved to the country to be near their mother recovering in a tuberculosis sanitarium. Though it takes place in postwar Japan it parallels the inner feelings and beliefs of Japan as much now as when it was released in 1989. The world of Japanese folk beliefs is animism where anything living or dead could be enlivened by spirits. For Miyazaki, there are many of these spirits, even the mundane innocuous and commonplace as "dust bunnies" have spirits as the playful *makuro kurosuke* or soot sprites[2]. This is part of the charm of the film and why so many continue to enjoy it.

Miyazaki through *anime* introduces the culture of Japan and its Shinto and Buddhist religious systems. He reveals the belief system of the unseen world of beings that are among us, both benevolent and malevolent. These religious beliefs are evidence of the Japanese Worldview of animism, a world of spirits, and forces that interact with humans and nature.

Japanese Soil

[2] These dust bunnies appear again in *Spirited Away* where the soot sprites are called *susuwatari* (wandering soot).

29

We are concerned with not only various religious beliefs but also the worldview behind these beliefs. As we saw in the introduction, worldview lies at the core of culture at levels far deeper than cultural behavior, values, and beliefs.

To comprehend the soil of Japan, we have looked at the nature of religion in Japan and how that affects the day-to-day belief and practice of religion. In order to better shape our sowing the gospel in Japan we will try to understand how all these religious beliefs fit together in a more holistic, big-picture, framework.

In studying any system of religious beliefs an analytic framework is very necessary. How do we go about understanding all individual beliefs and how they relate to one another? For the purpose of this short book we have chosen to use the model of mission anthropologist Paul Hiebert to reflect on the system of religious beliefs of the Japanese (Hiebert 1982, 39).

The Flaw of the Excluded Middle

However, before we begin to look at that framework, we must recognize a major flaw for many of us in perceiving worldview.

In a groundbreaking article, that has become a classic, Hiebert describes his own personal struggle in evaluating religious phenomena, beliefs, and behavior. Being trained scientifically as an anthropologist he easily sees the world relating to empirical evidence of the natural world. His other training in theology permitted him to view the world theologically and see the supernatural world. "For me the middle zone did not really exist" (Hiebert 1999, 418). Hiebert's main point is that many Westerners, even those trained in theology, evaluate religious phenomena either from a theological approach or a scientific approach. The upward realm of Religion is concerned with God, angels, and demons. This is the realm of the supernatural, the sacred, private truth, other-worldly problems, acted on in faith and perceived by miracles and visions. The lower realm of science is concerned with the natural order. This is the realm of the secular, public truth, this-worldly problems. This is the material universe of humans, animals, plants, and matter acted on by knowledge and perceived by sight and experience.

"Western cultures tend to cut reality into two big slices: the natural and the supernatural - the secular and the spiritual" (Van Rheenen 1991, 56). This dichotomous either-or thinking means we think theologically of God, angels, and heaven and the realm of the other-worldly supernatural or we think "this-worldly" science of the material universe and nature in the realm of the natural. One example is illness. When confronted by illness we may often question whether it is caused by something medical science could determine or was it caused by Satan like Job's illness (Job 2:7) or Paul's thorn in the flesh (2 Cor 12:7). This dichotomy or chasm develops in our thinking and worldview which ignores what Hiebert has called the "excluded middle" (See Figure 2). This leaves in the middle of our worldview a large gap where spiritual beings and forces exist in between these supernatural and natural realms (Van Rheenen 1991, 57). Westerners often "exclude the middle level of supernatural but this-worldly beings and forces from their worldview" (Hiebert 1982, 43). Since this analysis and the release of Hiebert's article numerous missiologists and practitioners have quoted this article due to its impact on their missions thinking.

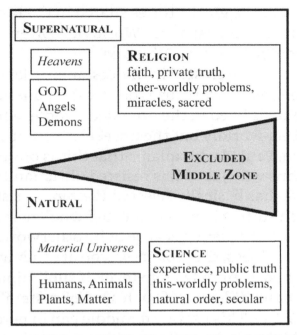

Figure 2 Hiebert 1999 The Flaw of the Excluded Middle

Communicating with Japanese

Because many Western missionaries and western trained Japanese view the world without this excluded middle, we have a difficult challenge of communicating the gospel in Japanese context to Japanese. "Missionaries exclude this middle realm and, consequently, are ill-prepared to communicate the gospel in animistic contexts where this realm is emphasized" (Van Rheenen 1991, 54).

The unseen or this-worldly supernatural side is extremely important to Japanese. This dichotomous thinking does not help us when we consider the ghost stories shared in the last chapter on the Japanese Worldview often presented by Hayao Miyazaki.

For us interested in understanding Japanese beliefs, we must realize that most Japanese religion is lived in the excluded middle, which is the this-worldly but the unseen or supernatural world. Paul Clark explains that this is one of the reasons why Japan has resisted Christianity. "Japan has basically rejected *Western* Christianity which suffers from a truncated wholeness, being a virtual dualism. Because of its otherworld centeredness, the Japanese, who are this-world oriented, cannot fathom (even if subliminally) the reasonableness of such a belief system" (Clark 1986, 29). This excluded middle gap in perceiving worldview creates problems in evangelizing Japanese. "While denial of the spiritual world leads to syncretism, acceptance of the spiritual world on its own terms leads to despair and bondage" (Bennett 2013, 146). Those sowing the gospel must learn to understand where Japanese are in their worldview and explain the Christian gospel in ways that address Japanese needs and questions.

Christian Foundations

Before we move on to the details of the analytic framework it would be good to briefly outline the Christian worldview. Our understanding of Christian theology or theism is

34

that God through special revelation has revealed to us our world and how to relate to him.

As Christians we do believe in supernaturalism which includes the existence of God himself a living unchangeable spirit being. Personal spiritual beings like angels exists; and miracles, violations of natural law, do actually occur. We live in a supernatural world where this all take place.

The Christian worldview, or theism, is based on several theological beliefs including these:

- The infinite immortal trinitarian God is the creator of the universe both of the natural world, included man, and all spiritual forces.
- Man was created by God as a unique creation with a spirit made in the image of God himself.
- God reigns in complete sovereign control of his creation that God guides and preserves.
- God is omnipotent, all-powerful, and almighty, over all of creation.
- God is a moral God who allows people the freedom to choose allegiance.
- Salvation can only be accomplished by God himself who alone is holy.

God Nearness and Distance

God continues in relationship with his created order, God is near and yet distant. God is present and active in his universe (immanence) and in other aspects he is separate and independent from the created order (transcendence). Together the immanence and transcendence of God means that God is a powerful and active personal God in our universe.

God's immanence means God, being omnipresent (Ps 139:1-10), is present in his creation (Jer 23:24) which he sustains (Job 34:14-15). Nature is totally dependent on God (Ps 104:29-30). God is continually revealing himself in nature through general revelation. The Holy Spirit is present in the earth convicting the world of sin, righteousness, and judgment (John 16:8).

God's transcendence means God is independent and distant from his creation. God is holy unlike the rest of creation and he possesses a majesty or "otherness" (Isa 6:1-5). "By this we mean that God is separate from and independent of nature and humanity. God is not simply attached to, or involved in, his creation. He is also superior to it" (Erickson 1985, 312). Yet God is active in sustaining, preserving, and working in his creation. The reality of Christianity is that there is an "other-worldly" place, heaven the throne of God. There are tremendous blessings for believers in Christ now and after death.

So this means that the Christian supernatural worldview is both very unlike what we experience on earth and at the same time is heaven-like. But this supernatural world is also "right with us" through visits of angels, the communion of the Holy Spirit, and the presence of God (Isa 41:10). God is complete in love (1 John 4:8) for all his creatures. As humans we can never capture completely the concept of God. God is the "wholly other."

> For my thoughts are not your thoughts, neither are your ways my ways," declares the Lord. "As the heavens are higher than the earth, so are my ways higher than your ways and my thoughts than your thoughts (Isa 55:8-9).

God's holiness, eternity, and omnipotence means he is transcendent. Which means "God is never fully within our grasp since he goes far beyond our ideas and forms, yet he is always available to us when we turn to him" (Erickson 1985, 319). Because God is also imminent. Christian believers are assured of the presence of the Holy Spirit, God's intimacy with them (John 14:16-18).

The Bible and the Excluded Middle

But Christianity also believes in the supernatural unseen beings and powers that are also immediate with us. There is this middle zone of angels and demons which can visit earth and influence humans.

This world of unseen spiritual forces were clearly understood in the Bible in the Old

Testament (Deut 32:17), throughout the gospels (Mark 5:1-17), seen in the Book of Acts (Acts 26:17-18), and in the letters to the churches of the New Testament (1 Tim 4:1). For example, Paul describes the rulers, authorities, powers of this dark world and spiritual forces of evil in the heavenly realms (Eph 6:10-12). Paul is speaking of the various evil forces led by Satan to oppose the Kingdom of God. Paul also speaks of the "elementary principles" (Gal 4:3 ESV) or *stoicheia* (cf. Col 2:8, 20) the spiritual forces that turn cultures from God and are active in various structures of human society distorting them (Van Rheenen 1991, 101). Five times the term "heavenly realms" is used in Ephesians and speaks of spiritual forces aligned against Christ and His reign (Eph 1:3, 20; 2:6; 3:10; 6:12).

Evil Satan and his minions do not have the power God has (Eph 1:9-10). They are all created beings, though fallen, and cannot overcome God. These spiritual beings which pose as gods will be thwarted and conquered by God himself. "These gods, who did not make the heavens and the earth, will perish from the earth and from under the heavens" (Jer 10:11).[3]

---

[3] For more on spiritual resistance and warfare see my other book, (Mehn 2017, 17-24).

Worldwide Influence of Japanese Beliefs

As followers of Christ we must watchful that eastern beliefs and worldwide influence do not erode our Christian Worldview. Our posture should be engagement in understanding *ki, feng shui*, astrology, and new age spirituality in our context and ultimately responding in the light of the proper understanding of biblical truth.

Outside of Japan the popularity of Japanese pop culture through manga, *anime*, and even themes in popular movies has widespread influence like Hayao Miyazaki and Studio Ghibi. An earlier interest in Eastern religion and philosophy and New Age spirituality is also cross-pollinating with these beliefs even in the West.

3

A Model for Understanding Japanese Beliefs

Now that we have explored the "flaw of the excluded middle" we can present Hiebert's framework of understanding religious beliefs. We need an analytic framework that does not ignore the excluded middle but helps us understand the worldview beliefs of Japanese. For any culture and worldview, Hiebert has developed a model, which places beliefs in two dimensions (see Figure 3).

Analytical Framework of Beliefs

TRANSCENDENCE

	ORGANIC Analogy	MECHANICAL Analogy	
	Cosmic Beings	Cosmic Forces	Other Worldly
Unseen or Supernatural	Local gods Spirits and Ancestors	Magic & Astrology	This Worldly
Seen or Natural	Folk Social Science	Folk Natural Science	

IMMANENCE

Figure 3 Adapted from Hiebert et al 1999 page 49

The first, or vertical dimension is transcendence and immanence. On the one hand, **immanence** is the empirical world of our senses in which we are constantly aware, and humans aim to explain this world and endeavor to control it. People through experimenting and observing learn how to live with nature and human relationships.

More remote from the seen world are those unseen beings and forces that cannot be conceived by our senses but are believed close at hand. These consist of angels, demons, ghosts, ancestors, local gods, spirits, and others that do not live in another world or time but immanently in this-world with humans on earth. Supernatural forces like magic, astrology, and divination also are included in this immanent or this worldly level. These are all "close at hand." In the film *My Neighbor Totoro* the titular character is local and immanent. He is a *yōkai* or forest god protecting the girls in the story. He is immediate to the characters and is their "neighbor."

On the other hand, *transcendence*, is the other-worldly level. This level is above sensory experience and is based on supernatural experiences of cosmic beings and forces beyond our human experience that exist on other-worlds or in other times (Hiebert 1982, 40-41).

The second, or horizontal dimension, uses two metaphors of organic or mechanical on a continuum. On the left side is the organic analogy of personal beings and on the right side is the mechanical analogy of impersonal forces.

The organic metaphor on the left is relational or a connection with personal beings. These are living beings in relationship with each other (Hiebert 1999, 417). These beings are believed to have a life of their own with feelings, thoughts, morals, and will (Hiebert 1999, 46-47). This includes cosmic beings as well as local gods, spirits, angels, demons, ghosts, ancestors, and others.

The mechanical metaphor on the right is deterministic or how individuals control impersonal forces (Hiebert 1982, 41-42). These are inanimate objects like parts of larger mechanical systems. They are controlled by impersonal forces and laws of nature (Hiebert 1999, 417). These impersonal forces such as luck, karma, magic, and divination are amoral, without feelings, or will.

We have first in this analytical framework the vertical dimension of transcendence and immanence. And we have seen the horizontal dimensions of beings (organic metaphor) and forces (mechanical metaphor). The framework seen from the top to bottom is divided into three levels, 1) other worlds – unseen and supernatural 2) this world – unseen or supernatural, and 3) this world – seen or natural (Hiebert et al 1999, 47-48). This reveals six distinct sectors in the analytical framework.

Japanese Religious Belief Systems

A preliminary example of applying this analytical framework to summarizing Japanese religious beliefs appears in (figure 4). You can see that Japanese religious beliefs cover all of the six sectors of the framework.

The Japanese Religious Belief System

TRANSCENDENCE

	ORGANIC Analogy	MECHANICAL Analogy	
	Amida Buddha	Karma Fate	Other Worldly
Unseen or Supernatural	Shinto gods The *kami* Buddhist gods The Departed Malevolent Beings	Chinese Magic Astrology Divination Charms & Amulets	This Worldly
Seen or Natural	Living gods Animals Plants	Chinese Medicine	

IMMANENCE

Figure 4

Comments on the Framework

Before we look in detail at all the dimensions and levels of Japanese beliefs, evaluating this model and its application in the Japanese context merits some brief comments and reminders.

First, as this is only an analytical model, it is best to not consider categories hard and fast. Moreover, as mentioned in chapter 1, Japanese religious beliefs can challenge even the notion of any categories. "One interesting characteristic of the Japanese folk beliefs we have explained is the fluidity of supernatural concepts; continua, rather than well-demarcated categories, constitute the supernatural world" (Befu 1971, 112). Often there is so much interconnectedness with various beliefs in this framework. *bachi* or

45

punishment can be either karmic or a personal punishment from a spiritual being. Japanese acquire power from an *o-mamori* charm to counter the karmic effects of *yakudoshi* or bad years. Though understanding this framework can be helpful for our understanding, we should use these categories and dimensions loosely.

Japanese religious beliefs would challenge categories of this analytical model, for example the organic metaphor and the mechanical metaphor can both be true. Some elements of Japanese religion appear to be mechanical or impersonal aspects of folk beliefs. Even the *butsudan* or Buddhist altar, the *kamidana* or Shinto god shelf, the *mamori* or safety charm (Lewis 2013, 13-16), and the *ihai* or memorial tablet (Yamaguchi 1985, 45) are viewed as a source of spiritual power and are believed by some to contain a spirit being.

Second, regarding the vertical or transcendence - immanence dimension, the Japanese religious belief system has blurred the distinctives between these upper and lower frames. For many Japanese there is only one single reality rather than two. Solheim defines this Japanese Worldview as "close to cosmological monism" (1984, 215) a belief in a oneness or single reality. "Cosmological monism is characterized by a single cosmos which includes both human beings and gods" (Solheim 1984,

214). Japanese religion is basically an immanence or a "close at hand" worldview. Solheim differentiates the Japanese religious culture as immanentist where the man-nature orientation is one in subjugation to or in harmony with nature. This is over against transcendentalist religious cultures where man is in mastery over nature (1984, 214). This is supported by Netland's view of Shinto where it is not "clear that the notion of religious ultimacy is even applicable in the case of Shinto, for the *kami* are not regarded as ontologically distinct from the phenomenal world. Strictly speaking the *kami* are not transcendent, standing over against the world, but rather exist with the continuum of the phenomenal world" (Netland 1991, 107). So the Japanese core cultural beliefs do not see much distinction between *kami* (gods), people, living things, and the dead, but are all closely connected.

Third, the distinct categories of natural and supernatural are also blurred. Netland says, "there is ... no clear ontological distinction between the natural realm and the supernatural realm" (Netland 1991, 101). Lewis conducted surveys with Japanese on the relationship of man to nature and the divine. Over 63% believed in a being above man and nature. But at the same time a large percentage also believed in a being contained within man and nature (Lewis 2013, 217-20). While for some Japanese they see a clear distinction between the divine and men, though for others this man-divine distinction is blurred and unclear. "Men are presently in the state of *kami*-hood. The Japanese word for this is *tenjin-goitsu* (unity of heaven and man)" (Corwin 1972, 159).

Analytic Framework of Japanese Beliefs

Using Hiebert's analytic framework we have developed one including many aspects of Japanese beliefs. This model does not neglect elements of the excluded middle which will help us better understand the overall worldview beliefs of Japanese (see Figure 5). This chart is a summary or a view of the forest from 30,000 feet, later we will look at the sections in detail and examine closeup on ground level even the types of trees. After some items is a code indicating the religious source of the belief whether it is primarily Shinto (S), Buddhist (B), Chinese religion (C).

A Model of the Japanese Religious Beliefs

TRANSCENDENCE

	ORGANIC Analogy	MECHANICAL Analogy	
	Amida Buddha (B)	Karma, Fate Koun (good luck) Kaiun (moral luck) Yakudoshi (unlucky years) (B) Lucky and unlucky days (B) Engi omen, portent (B), jinxes Ingo karmic cause (B)	Other Worldly
Unseen or Supernatural	Amaterasu, Izanagi, Izanami, and the Shinto Pantheon. (S) The kami (gods) (S) Bodhisattvas, Buddhas and the Buddhist pantheon. (B) Marebito (guests) Yurei (ghost of the departed) **The Departed** Kami (gods) (S) Senzo (ancestors) (S) Hotoke (buddhas) (B) Nii-botoke (new buddhas) (B) Shirei (spirits of the newly dead) (S) **Malevolent Beings** Goryo/ Onryo (malevolent spirits) (S) Gaki (hungry ghosts) (B) Bakemono or obake (ghost) (S) Tsukimono (possession by a spirit) (S) Bachi (punishment) (S) Mononoke (vagrant spirits) (S) Oni (demon, ogre) (S)	Yin-Yang Magic (C) Ki (life force) (C) Astrology Chinese (C) Astrology Western Numerology (C) Mediums Palmistry Ema (votive tablet) **Divination** Fortune telling (C) Geomancy (C) Seimei handan (Name divination) (S) Kokkuri Blood Group Divination **Charms & Amulets** o-mamori (amulet) (S) o-fuda (talisman) (S)	This Worldly
Seen or Natural	Ikigami (S) (human deity) Ikibotoke (B) (living gods) Animals (S) Plants (esp. sacred trees) (S) Nature (esp. mountains) (S)	Acupuncture (C) Chinese Medicine (C)	

IMMANENCE

Adopted from *Understanding Folk Religion* by Hiebert, Shaw, Tienou 1999. Used by Permission.

Figure 5

The Influence of Religious Traditions

Returning to our analytical model, how do we understand these religious beliefs in relation to each other? More importantly how can we understand the Japanese religious belief system as a part of the Japanese worldview? As we look at the details of Japanese religious beliefs in figure 5, we can see the influence of Shinto, Buddhist, and Chinese religious beliefs. These sources and roots of Japanese religion will be discussed in further chapters.

To summarize, the religious center of Japan is Shinto. This is an extension of religion directly into the culture according to Nakane and her classic book *Japanese Society*. "Japanese culture has no conception of a God existing abstractly, completely separate from the human world. In the ultimate analysis, the Japanese consciousness of the object of religion devotion grows out of direct-contact relations between individuals" (1970, 145). So from the vantage point of Shinto, the entire belief system would primarily contain the organic or personal this-worldly dimension of Shinto gods, the *kami*, the departed and nature. If Shinto religion alone were analyzed there would be no transcendent beings or forces as Shinto is basically unconcerned with the manipulation of mechanical forces; without the adaptation of other religious beliefs from Buddhism and Chinese religion the mechanical side would be absent.

Chinese religious belief systems have contributed very little to the personal aspect of religion or beings. There are no Chinese gods that the Japanese have adopted apart from those assimilated from Chinese Buddhism itself. Nearly all the contributions from Chinese religious belief systems are related completely to the mechanical aspects of the world. The Buddhist contribution has basically been in cosmology and "other worldly" aspects.

In this chapter we have presented a model of understanding religious beliefs. We have shared the six sectors of Japanese religious beliefs. The entire view from 30,000 feet has been presented. In this next chapter we will discuss details of each of these six individual sectors of the chart.

4

Understanding Japanese Religious Beliefs

Having introduced an overall model for understanding Japanese religious beliefs, we will now survey in brief each of the six sectors of this framework. We will move from the view of the forest to more tree top level and even identify some of the trees.

Room does not permit us to study all of them in detail, but we hope to present examples of popular religion beliefs and practices. Subsequently we will consider how specific Japanese religious beliefs and activities fit into these helpful dimensions and levels of this model. With each sector we will touch on possible implications of these beliefs for the Christian Worldview. Again the source of religious belief is listed as Shinto (S), Buddhist (B), or Chinese religion (C). Some readers not interested in all this detail may want skip ahead to the next chapter.

ORGANIC ANALOGY	
Unseen or Supernatural	Amida Buddha (B)

Figure 6

The first sector is beings that are transcendent unseen and other worldly. As mentioned earlier, in considering the big picture of the Japanese belief system, Japanese religion does not really have a concept of transcendent unseen beings. Maybe this sector should be left blank though for Japanese there only is one other-worldly cosmic being which would be unseen and supernatural. The Amida Buddha is only believed in certain branches of Mahayana Buddhism, such as the Pure Land or *Jōdo Bukkyō* sect in Japan (Earhart 2004, 101). Other Buddhist groups such as Nichiren actually oppose the concept of Amida Buddha as the center of Buddhist belief (Earhart 2004, 105).

Christian Worldview Implications

As shared earlier, the Christian Worldview places great emphasis on the creator God being transcendent. However, explaining greatness, magnificence, the creator, and all-powerful personal God to Japanese remains difficult. Those who are already exposed to a concept of a transcendent unseen being or have those beliefs would be easier to evangelize. Contextualizing and expanding those beliefs to include the creator, sovereign God of the Bible could be one of the next steps.

Mechanical Analogy
Karma, Fate
Koun (good luck)
Kaiun (moral luck)
Yakudoshi (unlucky years) (C)
Lucky and unlucky Days (C)
Engi omen, portent (B), jinxes,
Inga karmic cause (B)

Figure 7

Now when we approach other-worldly unseen and supernatural forces, the Japanese belief system has many mechanical forces and powers that affect their daily life. Much of this comes over from Chinese beliefs and are emphasized by Hindu-Buddhist concepts of Karma and Fate.

Some luck is deterministic in the nature of the event and amoral in nature like *kōun* or good luck or fortune. "In the framework of practical benefits, little is said about *kōun* because good luck has nothing to do with deliberate effort. But *kaiun* is the opposite: luck affected in even created by morality and religious ritual" (Reader & Tanabe 1998, 110). *Fuku* (luck or fortune) and *innen* or *kaiun* (moral luck) are impersonal cosmic forces (Reader & Tanabe 1998, 108-15) like *unmei* (destiny or fate). This sector also includes *inga,* karmic cause and effect, and omens, portents, and jinxes (Lewis 2013, 219).

One good example of this type of Japanese belief is *yakudoshi* (unlucky years) which is based on when you are born. There are predetermined years when the person would be most likely to meet with misfortune (Reader 1991, 29). *Yakudoshi* is widely believed in Japan leading to the practices of shrine visits and purchasing charms to avoid calamity (Lewis 2013, 119-31). A related belief is lucky and unlucky days on the Buddhist calendar (Lewis 2013, 97-98).

Christian Worldview Implications
The concept of karma, fate, or luck in its many forms is antithetical to the biblical view of God. The Japanese oft-used phrase *shikata ga nai* or "it cannot be helped" reveals the fatalistic understanding of their role in the world. In the Christian Worldview an all-powerful and all-ruling creator God relates intimately to human beings he created. He can protect them from calamity or give them strength through suffering.

ORGANIC ANALOGY		
Unseen or Super-natural	*Amaterasu, Izanagi, Izanami,* & the Shinto Pantheon. (S) The *kami* (gods) (S) *Bodhisattvas, Buddhas* & the Buddhist pantheon. (B) *Marebito* (guests) *Yurei* (ghost of the departed) **The Departed** *Kami* (gods) (S) *Senzo* (ancestors) (S) *Hotoke* (buddhas) (B) *Nii-botoke* (new buddhas) (B) *Shirei* (spirits of the newly dead) (S)	This Worldly

Figure 8

This sector of beliefs includes this-worldly beings unseen or supernatural and includes the Shinto pantheon of beings including the *kami*, the Buddhist pantheon of beings, ghosts, the departed, and malevolent beings. These are beings of the excluded middle that we discussed in chapter two.

Shinto pantheon - The Shinto pantheon contains many gods, but some notable ones mentioned in the *Kojiki* are *Izanagi* and *Izanami* the god and goddess that from their marriage union formed the islands of Japan. *Izanagi* later gave birth to *Amaterasu Ōmikami* (the sun goddess). The Emperors of Japan are said to be descendants of *Amaterasu*.

There are reputed to be 8 million gods or an uncountable number of *kami* in the Shinto belief system. *Kami* are spiritual beings that inspire awe by displaying superior power which can be seen as gods or spirits that exist in animate objects like animals, trees, mountains, boulders, rivers, and even humans. The *kami* will be discussed more in the next chapter.

The influence of State Shinto and the emperor system *tennōsei* has a profound impact on the identity of the Japanese people as well as their religious beliefs and is a far bigger topic than the scope of this book. The role of the Japanese emperor was changed after World War II and by constitution the role of the emperor remains only as a symbol of the state. But some consider the emperor to be an *ikigami* or a living God.[4]

At the time of this writing, the Imperial Household agency is preparing for a Shinto religious ceremony to be performed on the new Reiwa Emperor as part of his enthronement ceremonies. The *Daijosai* or the Great Thanksgiving Rite (Fujisawa 1958, 110-17; Ellwood 2008, 23-25), possibly the oldest state rite, will be held November 14-15, 2019. In the ceremony the new emperor prays and consumes

---

4 For further study See Robert Lee Ed. 1995. ` Tokyo: Tokyo Mission Research Institute.

some of the sacred rice offering. Through this rite he becomes unified with *Amaterasu Ōmikami* consequently the new emperor becomes the intermediary connecting Amaterasu and the people of Japan. During this rite the emperor will also offer rice and sake to Imperial ancestors and other deities. The same ceremony was performed for the Heisei Emperor in November 1990 with some controversy due to a debate on the separation of religion and the state (Ellwood 2008, 25).

The Japanese belief system simply adapted Buddhist entities to fit with their accepted number of deities. This includes *Bodhisattvas, Buddhas* and others of the Buddhist pantheon who have attained enlightenment and strive to help humans.

Marebito or (guests) are spirit beings that manifest themselves as travelers and appeal to humans for hospitality. They bring luck and other blessings to those who care for them. (Kodansha 1993, 923).

Yūrei are ghosts or phantoms of the departed (Kodansha 1993, 454) who can become malevolent if proper rites are not performed (see next section).

The Departed - A special word should be said about unseen supernatural beings in this world related to the departed. The terminology used to describe different kinds of spirits has many local and individual variations. Lewis (1993, 65) and Dore (1958, 435) in their field research found that most people could not differentiate between various words for spirit, soul and other terms that speak of the departed. Various Shinto terms are used interchangeably for the soul, spirit, or god such as *kami, mitama, rei*, and *shinrei*. And various Buddhist terms are used interchangeably for the soul or spirit: *hotoke, tamashi, reikon, rei*. In Japanese religion it is believed that the souls of the dead follow stages in regular progression from *shirei* (spirits of the newly dead) to *nii-botoke* (new buddhas) to *hotoke* (buddhas) to *senzo* (ancestors) to ultimately *kami* (god), though often the order and use of these terms vary (Lewis 2018, 276).[5]

Christian Worldview Implications

The Christian Worldview is based on the Scriptural teachings of God, Christ, and his work for us through the cross and the resurrection. Scriptural teachings related to the state of the eternal soul after death is what is traditionally called personal eschatology. In Christianity the view of death is always related to the cross and the resurrection of Christ. One view is that the soul after death is sent by God to an immediate state called "paradise" for fellowship with Christ

---

[5] Compare field research of (Dore 1958, 431-435), (Plath 1964, 301-4), (Smith 1974, 56), and (Lewis 1993, 64).

(2 Cor 5:8). Souls of non-believers are sent by God to *sheol* or *hades* (death). Both believers and unbelievers await the return of Christ and the final resurrection where their immortal souls will be reunited with their resurrected bodies before the Final Judgment. This will be discussed more in depth in chapter five related to Japanese view of ancestor worship.

ORGANIC ANALOGY		
	Malevolent Beings	
Unseen or Super-natural	*Goryo/ Onryo* (malevolent spirits) (S) *Gaki* (hungry ghosts) (B) *Bakemono or obake* (ghost) (S) *Tsukimono* (possession by a spirit) (S) *Bachi* (punishment)(S) *Mononoke* (vagrant spirits) (S) *Oni* (demon, ogre) (S)	This Worldly

Figure 9

The Japanese belief system comprises a large range of "This-worldly" unseen malevolent beings that haunt and torment people in this world. These supernatural beings come from Shinto and Buddhist beliefs. They have led to many ghost stories, with in *Manga* and *anime* including Miyazaki's films.

Malevolent beings like *onryō* (malevolent spirits) and *goryō* (Ellwood 2008, 103; Hori 1968, 43-44) are *gaki* (hungry ghosts). A form of hungry ghost is the *muenbotoke or the* dead that are unattached with no relatives to perform rites after their death. People with few relatives are fearful of becoming a *muenbotoke* and the rite of *segaki* is performed during *obon* to appease them (Lewis 2018, 29). *Bakemono* or *obake* (ghost) are also terms for monster or goblin. These are generally termed *yōkai* (ghost/phantom). They may appear in non-human form as well as the wind, sounds or fire. (Kodansha 1993, 93). *Tsukimono* (possession by a spirit) can be living or dead spirits that possess people chiefly by animals such as a dog, fox or snake (Kodansha 1993, 1632). *Bachi* (divine punishment or curse or retribution) can also be seen as impersonal (or mechanical) punishment (see *karma, innen* above). *Mononoke* are vagrant spirits or specters that could be of the living or the deceased (Kodansha 1993,1002). These supernatural shape-shifting beings can possess individuals, make them suffer, or cause distress or even death. The *oni* is a demon or ogre and its statues often guard the entrances of temples and shrines. *Oni* are often associated with the *mamemaki* bean-scattering ceremony held at *setsubun* (Reader 1991, 34-35).

Christian Worldview Implications

Japanese strongly believe in the existence of these spiritual beings (see next chapter). From a Christian Worldview perspective, the concern for or fears of these beings could be influenced by "the spiritual forces of wickedness in the heavenly places" (NASB). The reality of evil spirits or demons should not be ignored when viewing these Japanese beliefs. We need to be reminded of Christ's victory over Satan and all his spiritual forces (Col 2:15) that will be studied in later chapters.

	MECHANICAL ANALOGY	
Unseen or Super-natural	Yin-Yang Magic (C) *Ki* (life force)(C) Astrology 'Chinese'(C) Astrology 'Western' Numerology (C) Mediums Palmistry *Ema* (votive tablet)	This Worldly

Figure 10

This sector contains unseen and supernatural forces like magic, *ki*, astrology, and the use of palmistry, numerology and mediums. These are forces and powers in this world that can be influenced and even controlled. They come from the influence of Taoism and Chinese religious beliefs.

Japanese believe and practice yin-yang or Chinese magic. They also believe in *ki* or life or vital force as a part of any living being. This vital force or *ki* must be balanced for good health and is the basis for Chinese traditional medicine and

63

acupuncture will discussed in the next chapter. In addition to the Japanese there is a strong element within new age religion which is more common in the West.

Astrology is a belief that celestial forces affect the destiny of humans on earth. The Japanese follow Chinese astrology (Lewis 2018, 120-21). As Western astrology continues to be the most common form of divination in the West (Van Rheenen 1991, 179) it is also popular in Japan (Lewis 2018, 119-20). Japanese continue to follow the zodiac sign to determine their personal characteristics or predict their future.

Divination is commonly practiced in Japan and will specifically be discussed below. The use of mediums for divination, including necromancy where the dead are called on behalf of the living to give guidance (Van Rheenen 1991, 184-85) is widespread (Lewis 2013, 148-51). You can find mediums and palmistry *tesō* (Lewis 2013, 136) all over Japan even in departments stores.

Visitors to shrines or temples use *ema* or votive tablets to write their petitions to *kami* or Buddhas on the votive tablet (Reader 1991 175-82). They could be seen by some as a means to coerce or force the *kami* to grant the visitor's wish or prayer (Reader & Tanabe 1998, 197-99).

MECHANICAL ANALOGY		
	Divination	
Unseen or Super- natural	Fortune telling (C) Geomancy (C) *Seimei handan* (Name divination) (C) *Kokkuri* Blood Group Divination	This Worldly
	Charms & Amulets	
	o-mamori (amulet) (S) *o-fuda* (talisman) (S)	

Figure 11

People are constantly seeking guidance for their lives. Often Japanese seek guidance from "this-worldly" unseen or supernatural forces and powers. A variety of practices influenced by Chinese religion manifest themselves under the broad heading of divination. Some of these are practiced widely and influence Christians which leads to syncretism or "split-level" Christianity (see chapter one).

Fortune telling or *uranai* can be both the divining of the future as well as testing fate. One type is by means of lots or written oracles (*o-mikuji*) (Ono 1962, 62 & Lewis 2013, 133-35). Visitors to temples and shrines purchase these divination slips and tie them to racks or trees as a means of spreading their petition with every wind (Reader & Tanabe 1991, 72; Lewis 2018, 116-18).

Geomancy *kasō* is the physical aspect of buildings or the physiognomy of a home. The *Kimon* or "devil's door" is the malicious direction of a home (Lewis 2018 138-40) so the practice of *hoigaku* or the art of facing houses in the proper direction (Dale 1975, 9) is practiced. Historically to protect homes or castles from evil spirits, shrines were often placed in the direction of the expected attack by these beings (Lewis 1993, 29). And there is a common belief that demons cannot walk around corners so in park walkways and even our front walk of our home is not in a straight line and contains right angles.

Seimei handan or name divination is a type of onomancy using the number of strokes in Chinese ideographs (*kanji*) to determine the best destiny of selecting a name for a newborn child (Lewis 2018, 92-95).

Kokkuri is a popular means of divination using a *Ouiji-* type board that contains all 52 characters of Japanese kana (Lewis 2018, 115-16).

Blood Group Divination (Lewis 2018, 121-22) - In the west it is convenient to know your blood group in case you need a transfusion or need to donate blood. In Japan some see it as convenient to know your blood group as it determines your personality and the kind of decisions you make.

Charms and Amulets are a form of apotropaic magic, to ward off misfortune. The *o-mamori* (amulet), also called a *gofu*, is for safety and protection. Lewis found that over 65% in his survey had at least one *mamori*. Some believe that the *mamori* only symbolizes a deity, but others believe that the *mamori* itself contains the deity (Lewis 1993, 33).

Another form of magic is the *o-fuda* (talisman). "*Fuda* are similar to *omamori* in that they too are regarded as manifestations ... of the sacred entity enshrined at the temple or shrine." (Reader & Tanabe 1998, 67). They are widely used for protection from misfortune and danger (Reader 1991, 184-90; Lewis 2018, 89). The *mayoke* are special talismans or rites, which expel demons and evil spirits. (Kodansha 1993, 940).

Christian Worldview Implications

The Christian Worldview is in sharp contrast with the Japanese Worldview reflected in this sector. Believers in Christ must acknowledge that a personal God of grace is intimately concerned for all aspects of one's life. The highest spiritual power is not an impersonal force, but our Heavenly Father who is loving and caring (Matt 10:29, 30). This loving God also sovereignly controls even the stars and planets as well as details of your life (Rom 8:28). This king is aware of you personally and is in control of every aspect of our life. This all-powerful, all-knowing and imminent God, as we trust and rely on him, will provide blessed guidance to us at all times (Ps 32:8). As our protector we do not need to seek any other source of protection.

	ORGANIC ANALOGY	MECHANICAL ANALOGY	
Seen or Natural	Ikigami (S) (human deity) Ikibotoke (B) (living gods) Animals (S) Plants (esp. sacred trees) (S) Nature (esp. mountains)(S)	Acupuncture (C) Chinese Medicine (C)	This Worldly

Figure 12

For the last sectors, here we see together the organic and mechanical analogies side by side. In both of these sectors is the seen or natural "this worldly" beliefs. We will look at the left side then in turn the right side.

This category of folk social science includes organic beings such as living gods and sacred nature from the traditions of Shinto and Buddhism (figure 12). *Ikigami* are human deities and *Ikibotoke* are living gods or Buddhas that is a living person that is revered as a god or *kami*. This is the basis for Japanese Emperor worship. Some founders of new religions insist a *kami* entered them and possessed them (Hori 1972, 97-99) making them an *ikigami*.

Some animals are believed to protect the graves of the departed. Animals are also seen as embodiments of spirits of the dead. For example, foxes are believed to be messengers of *inari* the god of cereals (Lewis 2013, 6-7). Unlike Christianity, Japanese Worldview believes that besides man other natural beings have spirits or souls. Plants especially sacred trees are spiritual in nature like in the film *My Neighbor Totoro*. Nature namely mountains, waterfalls, and rivers are also seen as spiritual.

This category of the forces of folk natural science are the seen and natural forces that occur in this world (on the right of figure 12). This sector of beliefs contains Chinese medicine and treatments like acupuncture. For acupuncture and its association with *ki* see the comments above. A discussion here about Chinese medicine and acupuncture is to establish the religious beliefs behind these practices and not to debate the efficacy of these treatments. As this view of medicine was born from another Asian worldview and belief system, they have a different worldview from that which birthed Western medicine.

Christian Worldview Implications

As stated earlier in the Christian Worldview the creator God continues to have a relationship with his creation. So the creation is unique and special not "sacred" in that is possessed by spirits. The creation revolves around the center of God's creation: man himself. He alone possesses the . Nature is intended to serve him as he governs and protects it.

Conclusion

To assist us in sharing the gospel in Japanese soil, in the last chapter we introduced an analytical framework for understanding Japanese religious beliefs, kind of a big picture view from 30,000 feet. In this chapter we have looked at details and various aspects of Japanese religious beliefs, kind of a closeup ground level look at each sector of the analytical framework. We tried to show how these beliefs fit together and interact. Readers should be reminded that this is just a model and not the last word on this extremely complicated topic.

We were introduced to the kind of beliefs that are challenging to address from the Christian Worldview for instance *kami*, karma, the ancestors, divination, and other spirit beings. For each sector of the model we included a brief summary from the Christian Worldview perspective.

In the next chapters we will continue to outline the Japanese soil by introducing the roots and sources of Japanese religious beliefs and how these are practiced in Japanese folk religion.

5

The Five Japanese Belief Systems

Japan is a living museum of religions[6]

Several years ago, I had the privilege to visit a home of a very prominent man in the community of Ishinomaki, Miyagi prefecture. He showed me the foremost room of his house that I would summarize as his "room of beliefs." This large room contained a Buddhist home altar or *butsudan*. In another section of the room was the prominent Shinto god shelf or *kamidana*. On one wall were the photographs of deceased relatives he identified to me as his own parents and grandparents. These photographs were the same black and white prints framed and used at their funerals. On another wall were several framed

---

[6]Earhart 1969, 1

formal commendations of thanksgiving (*kansha-jō*) to his father from The Imperial Household Agency and Emperor Showa. These signified his father's service in World War II as an imperial navy officer. In one room you could sense this important man's beliefs and an illustration of Japanese beliefs in Shinto, Buddhism, the Emperor, and his ancestors.

Most Japanese would readily identify themselves as believers of either Shintoism or Buddhism and often both. However, religious belief in Japan "is a variegated tapestry created by the interweaving of at least five major strands, Shinto, Buddhism, Daoism, Confucianism and folk religion" (Earhart 2014, 2). In many ways, these belief systems function as one and people typically move from Shinto ideas to Buddhist practices easily without much thought.

This chapter is a survey of the five streams of Japanese religious belief. We have reflected on individual beliefs in previous chapters but here we will study their traditions separately so that the overall influence of the religious tradition can be understood more in greater depth. We will begin with Shinto the roots of Japanese religion, then discuss Buddhism, Confucianism, Taoism, and finally Japanese Folk Religion. We will then explore briefly Japanese New Religions and New New Religions and close with some comments on the Japanese and secularization. We begin with the roots of Japanese religious beliefs, Shinto.

The Japanese Shinto Belief System

The major contributor to the Japanese religious belief system is Shinto. "Shinto is the spiritual bedrock of Japan" (Spae 1968, 9) and "at once the physical and metaphysical backbone of Japan" (Fujisawa 1958, 20) upon which the rest of religious beliefs are supported. This animistic system of the "way of the *kami*" considers the gods or spirits, powers, and forces occupying a region and indeed the whole nation of Japan. Of all the religious traditions in Japan, Shintoism is the most pervasive and influential. Joseph Spae, a missionary and religious researcher, encourages us to truly understand Shinto beliefs.

Westerners have found extreme difficulty in considering Shinto as anything other than an underdeveloped, animistic folk religion . . . Personally, I am opposed to the frequently heard thesis that Buddhism and Confucianism are more basic parts of Japan's spiritual civilization than Shinto. This neglect of Shinto is a distortion and needs correction . . . every tradition which succeeded in implanting itself in Japanese soil was affected by Shinto – and came to terms with it at some time or other (Spae 1968, 8).

We have discussed Shinto several times but here we will discuss a few aspects of Shinto as they relate to "nature-power," Shinto as a religion, the *kami*, and ancestors.

Shintoism is the Worship of Nature-power

Shintoism is the "most institutionalized form of man's kinship with nature" (Steyne 1990, 69). This worldview, as explained by Smart as cosmological monism, invokes "a powerful sense of the presence of gods and spirits in nature" (1969, 192). It is these natural and powerful forces in nature that are the object of worship and veneration.

One scene from the scene *My Neighbor Totoro* the images and symbols of Shinto are prominent when Dr. Kusakabe and his two girls go to pay respect to the sacred tree. This huge tree is wrapped in a *shimenawa* a rope used to separate consecrated areas. Off this rope are many *shide* or zigzag-shaped paper or cloth streamers that symbolize lightning. This is all symbolism of a part of nature that is sacred and powerful. Earlier in the film the father talks about the spirit of the tree and how it is an ancient powerful being of nature.

Shinto as a "Religion"

Even though Shinto is properly called *the way of the* gods, in a poll only 2% of Japanese listed Shinto as a religion. Having called this discrepancy to their attention then only 56% considered it a religion (Clark 1986, 26). Even while entering a Shinto shrine to conduct practices many would not consider themselves part of Shinto organized religion. This is due to the folk religious nature of Shinto itself. "There was neither an originator nor a sacred book. Neither was any systematic practice of Shinto in existence" (Uemura 2001, 9). In many ways to be Japanese is to be Shinto. Shinto is the essence of being Japanese. "In its general aspects *Shinto is more than a religious faith.* It is an amalgam of attitudes, ideas, and ways of doing things that through two millennia and more have become an integral part of the *way* of the Japanese people. Shinto is both a personal faith in the kami and a communal way of life according to the mind of the kami" (Ono 1962, 3). Shinto as an animistic religion is very hard to "nail down" and even harder to get Japanese to admit their beliefs. This all presents difficulties for us who are trying to share Christ's gospel and one particular difficulty is the Japanese concept of God.

The *Kami*

"The word *'kami'* defies definition, but from Shinto tradition generally means an 'elevated being' not above but within nature" (Corwin 1962, 19). Spiritual manifestations are capable from natural phenomena whether animate or inanimate even from man-made objects (Befu 1971, 101). The word *kami* "means any being that has unusual power of is exceedingly awe-inspiring or superior in potency" (Ross 1980, 313).

> among the objects or phenomena designated from ancient times as *kami* are the qualities of growth, fertility, and production; natural phenomena, such as wind and thunder; natural objects, such as the sun, mountains, rivers, trees and rocks; some animals; and ancestral spirits. In the last-named category are the spirits of the Imperial ancestors, the ancestors of noble families, and in a sense all ancestral spirits (Ono 1962, 7).

Shinto has a large pantheon of gods and *kami* of many types and varieties. "It was characteristic of earlier Japanese to deify everywhere; to see a god or godling in every kind of forces or natural object. Hence it was that they called their country 'the Land of the Gods,' and in later times estimated that their deities must number some 'eighty myriads' or even some 'eight hundred myriads'" (Ross 1980, 306). This "phrase should not be taken to be an enumeration of the actual number of *kami* so much as an indication that the *kami* are innumerable, ubiquitous, and the fountainhead of all life" (Netland 1991, 101).

The *kami* can be mythical deities such as *Amaterasu*, living persons, spirits of the living or the deceased, animals (especially foxes, dogs, and snakes), and plants (especially old trees). As the *kami* can be practically anything thus "the theological distinctions often made among gods, deities, souls, and spirits is irrelevant" (Befu 1971, 104). In regard to hierarchy among the *kami*, "the chief place in the pantheon was given to the sun-goddess, *Amaterasu*, ... but she has never been regarded as more than the first among her peers" (Ross 1980, 306). This prominence of *Amaterasu* can be seen in the connection of the Emperor and this goddess.

Many have discussed the use of the Japanese word *kami* to translate the Bible in an attempt to explain God. There is no room for a full discussion here, but one prominent Japanese pastor, during his entire career, refused to use the words *kami* or *kamisama* for the God of the Bible and instead used *sōzō-nushi* or "creator God." In any event, the word *kami* probably cannot be avoided due to history but must be modified with adjectives and further description so that Japanese can understand the transcendent nature of the Christian God. Ayabe advises that the word *"kami"* should not be used for the biblical God without using biblical adjectives along with it (Ayabe 1992, 102–03). Another important distinction is that the *kami* are not moral, whereas the Christian God is holy and pure, and God demands holiness and purity in relating to created humans (1 Tim 6:15-16).

The *kami* are actually seen as local dwelling gods that are "associated with a particular locale and identified with a unique abode" (Befu 1971, 103). Each family would have its own local clan god or *ujigami*. When entering their territory Japanese believe it is essential to appease these local gods to prevent misfortune. The purpose of the *jichisai* or groundbreaking ritual used before new construction begins on a piece of land is to appease the god that inhabits there (Lewis 2013, 25). Many homes also have another ritual when the roof joists are finally raised, again placating the local gods. Shinto beliefs are tied very much to the old Japanese agrarian society and culture. In many regions of Japan it is believed that the mountain *kami* may migrate in the spring becoming the rice field *kami*.

In Japanese mythology there are the *kami* of heaven (*ama-tsu-kami*) and the *kami* of the earth (*kuni-tsu-kami*) and these *kami* come and go between these two stations. The *kami* can also change roles especially when the old role is outdated. In some sense the location and the role of the *kami* is fluid (Befu 1971, 101-2). "Japanese believe that at death the spirit of the deceased, rather than immediately going to a far and radically different place, remains nearby, first near the body, then the grave and the memorial tablet" (Milhous 1984, 13). This deceased spirit can also be in two places at once wandering in the nearby mountains or the ocean but still residing in the *ihai* memorial tablet.

In this particular sense the *kami* are gods of immanence not transcendence. "The Shinto *kami* have never been conceived of as absolute or transcendent in relation to man and the world – not even in the case of *Izanagi, Izanami,* or *Amaterasu.* On the contrary, it has always been assumed that there is a significant continuity between the *kami* and man" (Ueda 1972, 33). The belief in *kami* has a close connection with the local clan, individuals, and the ancestors.

The Ancestors

Japanese ancestor worship differs from Chinese ancestor worship and it predates the introduction of Buddhism into Japan. The Shinto belief system supporting the belief in the *kami* also supports the belief that the ancestors still reside with the living and that they will eventually become *kami.* For the living that remain, "there is a general cognitive and emotional emphasis on those who have died within living memory, as compared with more distant ancestors who are eventually no longer distinguished by separate rites but are merged into the collectivity of the ancestors" (Lewis 2013, 47-48).

Ancestors are revered for many reasons. They have the priority of parenthood, as they are wiser, they possess special powers and achievements, and continue to be members of our family as long as they remain in our memory (Hiebert et al 1999, 119-22). Also ancestors have knowledge of the afterlife and communication with them such as divination (*uranai*) is practiced by reading signs from animals, dreams and shamanistic mediums (Kodansha 1993, 288).

Dore has described ancestor worship rites and their meaning in typical Japanese community life (1958, 317-25). The major function of ancestor worship in Japan is to reinforce the family ties between the living descendants and the dead ancestors. "Since the ancestors are dependent for the well-being and even their continued existence upon the ritual homage and veneration of those still living, and since the ancestors are able to intervene (for good or evil) in the affairs of the living, it is crucial that those still living give appropriate homage and veneration to the spirits of the deceased" (Netland 1985, 7). This is true from the average Japanese up to the emperor himself.

Those that are recently departed can, through a series of rites occurring at specific intervals of days and even years, become more and more a god. Ronan citing Ushijima says that "each rite in the funeral process moves the spirit of the dead upward as it becomes more purified, clearly suggesting that the deceased becomes 'sacred' through the funeral rituals by which they are 'set apart'" (Ronan 1999, 9). Most Japanese people believe that the spirit (*reikon*) is separated from the body and becomes a benevolent spirit, provided that the proper rituals are performed on its behalf (Mullins 1998, 247). The deceased begin as a spirit of the newly dead (*shirei*), then a 'new buddha' (*nii-botoke*) into a *senzo* (ancestor) or *hotoke* (buddha) and finally into a *Hotoke* (Buddha) or *kami* (god) (Lewis 2013, 47).[7]

Those who have died in battle, political intrigues, accidents, miscarried or aborted fetuses (*mizuko*) or by suicide are of a particular concern to Japanese. These are people who have died "bad deaths" and are filled with resentment and hatred (Hori 1968, 121). In the past Japanese "people were afraid of spirits of the dead, who preyed on them. All social and personal crises ... were believed to be the result of the vengeance of angry spirits of the dead." (Hori 1968, 72 & 123) This is still true today.

After the triple disaster of earthquake, tsunami, and nuclear disaster in 2011, the

---

[7] For these details see also the discussion in the previous chapter.

numbers of those reported dead were over 18,000 people. These were ones who died "bad deaths" and according to Japanese beliefs there is a great concern over the number of ghosts and spirits of the dead that could come and haunt the living with misfortune. Even a year after the disaster many media outlets were reporting stories and the widespread fear of ghosts in the disaster area. One university researcher was investigating the "continuing bonds" of the deceased and the living as a means of dealing with grief and providing security to individuals.

Those who have died "bad deaths" are *muenbotoke* or nameless and unknown spirits. "The suffering of the spirit is compounded by its isolation from other spirits. Thus, most suffering spirits soliciting human help are also identified as *muen* ('lonely, affinity-less') spirits. A spirit is *muen* not only because of its *tsumi* [sin] but because it has been neglected or abandoned by human survivors" (Lebra 1976, 238). If these nameless spirits (*muenbotoke*) do not have the proper rites performed on their behalf they could become (*goryō* or *onryo*) vengeful spirits of the dead (Antoni 1993, 125; Lewis 2013, 1). These *onryo* can take out vengeance (*urami*) on people leaving them with cursing and misfortune (*tatari*) and generating feelings of fear

Another aspect related to the deceased that brings fear is *bachi* (divine punishment, retribution or a curse), which can include just the transgressor or an entire group such as a household. Over half surveyed by David Lewis believe they would suffer divine punishment if they were to do something bad (2013, 220). The concepts of *bachi* vary quite a bit from individual to individual. Usually it is perceived as guilt or a misfortune such as an accident or illness. Some believe it results from neglecting your ancestors, bad conduct, problems in human relationships like betrayal, and certain taboos (Lewis 2013, 220-21).

The Japanese Buddhistic Belief System

Another major source for Japanese beliefs is Buddhism. Originally from India, Buddhism passed through China and Korea before arriving in Japan during the sixth century. Although transplanted from the outside, Buddhistic belief systems that entered Japan have undergone severe transformation to become Japanese in both philosophy and practice. "Some scholars go so far as to say that Japanese Buddhism is not real Buddhism at all or at best a deformed version" (Hori 1968, 83). So the Buddhism that exists in Japan today "is a strongly Japanese-colored Buddhism that in many respects is different from traditional Buddhism" (Solheim 1984, 215). The "Great Vehicle" or Mahayana Buddhism arose in Japan with five major schools of Tendai, Shingon,

Jōdo, Zen and Nichiren along with many sub-sects.

In Japan the strong and encompassing Shinto belief in the *kami* was hard to reconcile with the divine understanding within Buddhism and led to many adaptations. "Within the Shinto-Buddhist syncretic systems (*honji suijaku*) ... particular Shinto *kami* were associated with particular Buddhist divinities and thus transformed in important ways. Attempts to establish an all-encompassing *kami* at the very top of the pantheon failed" (Kodansha 1993, 727). But for the average Japanese the "*kami* are seen as *bodhisattvas* or manifestations of Buddha" (Hiebert & Meneses 1995, 215).

There were many elements of Buddhism which contributed to the overall Japanese religious belief system. "Buddhism furnished philosophy, cosmology, rituals, objects of worship, and formulas" (Earhart 1969, 55). The belief in *Amida*, Buddha of Light, has led to several major branches of Buddhism in Japan as well as some new religious elements (Iglehart 1957, 24). But the most important contribution to a belief system in Japan is Buddhism's treatment of death and transiency (Lee 1999, 69).

Karma or fate is the core tenant of Buddhism. "One of the great attractions of Buddhism lies in its offer of a wide variety of humanly available methods for getting rid of bad karma (*metsuzai*) for the past and establishing good karma for the present and the future" (Reader & Tanabe 1998, 111).

There are six stages in Buddhist hell, the first being the "Inferno of Starvation" or *gaki* where all the spirits are starved. In order to progress to the next level certain rites must be performed for the deceased. In Buddhist hell "there is the dreaded *"Ema Tai-o"* with his blue and red demons to torture the dead (Luke 1970, 65).

However, for many Japanese "ideas of transmigration and of nirvana have never been a part of the Buddhist faith of the people.... they have never affected folkways of popular thought" (Benedict 1946, 237-238). There are many other aspects of traditional Buddhism which have been rejected by the Japanese belief systems such as the Buddhist concept of rewards and punishments. Buddhism led to many more beliefs and practices which were adopted, modified, or rejected by Japanese religion. The elements and how they were integrated in Japan leave a complicated religious landscape.

The Japanese Confucianism Belief System

Another headwater for religious beliefs was China. For years the cultural exchanges between Japan and China formed places for formal and folk religious beliefs to interact. Two religious' systems of beliefs and practices from China began to influence Japan (Earhart 2004, 52-65). Confucianism entered Japan between the sixth and ninth century from Korea and China. About this time Buddhism was also being imported and overshadowed Confucianism. Due to the adoption of Buddhist religious systems, the Confucian role in Japanese society is limited to social ethics. The Japanese observed the highly ordered Chinese society and viewed Confucianism "as a basic model on which to pattern other social relationships, a prototype of social organization" (Tomikura 1972, 111). The feudal period of the Tokugawa Era (1603-1868) brought an increased desire for strong social order, so Confucianism was sought to meet that need. Confucianism consequently has a great influence on Bushido or the "way of the warrior" the code of conduct for the Samurai.

The influence of Confucianism in Japan is far-reaching; however, Confucianism could be better viewed as a social ethical system not as a religion. The feudal and hierarchical society was reinforced through Confucian social ethics (Earhart 2004, 147). Confucianism was the basic model to pattern other social relationships such as the family (Tomikura 1972, 111) and "has become universalized as the normative social identity for all Japanese" (Lee 1999, 69). Consequently, Reischauer has asserted, "Almost no one considers himself a Confucianist today, but in a sense almost all Japanese are" (1978, 214). The concept of filial piety comes directly from Confucianism and is the ethical foundation that supports the ancestor cult. However, though Confucianism has contributed much in the semi-sacred area of family life (Iglehart 1957, 68), little has been contributed in the area of belief systems.

The Japanese Taoism Belief System

Another stream from China was Taoism (or Daoism). Though not as prominent as a religion, Taoism "penetrated deeply into the folk belief systems and practices" of the Japanese (Davies 2016, 79). In Japan, other elements of Chinese religion that were introduced were *yin-yang* magic and techniques of Taoism (Hori 1968, 9). Taoism never became a formal religion in Japan but in the seventh century the *onmyō-dō* (the way of the Yin and Yang) sect became part of the Japanese religious climate. Its contributions to belief systems were "some philosophical, astrological, animistic, and magical theories and practices" (Hori 1968, 79). The practitioners of the *onmyō-dō* sect, "engaged in such matters as divination, astrology, and fortune-telling. *onmyō-dō* became intermingled with Shinto and thus merged imperceptibly into the popular beliefs which spread all over Japan" (Hori 1968, 79). The influence of Taoism on Shintoism and Buddhism continues today and *onmyō-dō* is the source of the popularity of numerology, auspiciousness of certain days, and lucky and unlucky directions (Kodansha 1993, 1149).

Some Japanese believe in *ki* (or in Chinese c*h'i* or *qi*) or energy life force a belief borrowed directly from China. This force is believed to enter the body at birth and leave at death. This is the basis for the use of acupuncture, which believes in 365 points where acupuncture can affect the flow of *ki* in the body (Lewis 1993, 158).

The belief in *ki* also is the basis for geomancy divination. "*Qi* is a force in the Chinese philosophy of space known as geomancy or *feng shui*...all persons are linked to nature, and that their well-being depends on their living in harmony with it. Misfortune is attributed to the lack of a happy alignment with the surrounding terrain" (Hiebert et al 1993, 139). This is the belief system behind the practices of *kasō* (the physiognomy of the house) in finding the *kimon* (devil door) or the malicious direction of an entrance. The Chinese idea of the human body being a small manifestation of the entire universe leads to several medical practices and also religious rites (Corwin 1972, 110-11).

Japanese Folk Religion

Though Shinto, Buddhism, Confucianism, and Taoism have played their roles in Japanese religion, the prevailing system of beliefs or religious practices in Japan resides not primarily in organized religion. Japanese are averse to organized religion and poll accordingly. On the other hand, Japanese continue to be an extremely spiritual people and on a folk level many Japanese are practicing religion at fairly high numbers (Netland 2015, 68) as we will show in the next chapter.

As was said earlier, Japanese religion is often unstructured, defies analysis, adapts by making use of many elements, and is intensely practical which fits folk religion with its adaptions and hodgepodge of practices. It is in folk religion, where a blend of religious and quasi-religious elements come to meet the needs of everyday Japanese (Hori 1968, xi).

Folk religion serves to answer some of the deepest concerns of the beliefs and practices of a people. Hiebert, Shaw, and Tienou in their book *Understanding Folk Religion* outline the four major existential questions of everyday life and concerns for power and success (1999, 77-79).

1. The meaning of life and the problem of death. Death brings grief and meaninglessness to those living who experience the death of others.
2. Well-being in this life and the problem of misfortunes. Man desires a good fulfilling life of health, family, food, and shelter. Other people seek power, status, wealth,

and success. All people face the threat of
loss, failure, trouble, disaster, and other
misfortunes. What is the basis for this
misfortune and what are the means of
securing well-being in life?
3. The knowledge to decide and the problem
of the unknown. There are many ways
people seek guidance in life and find ways
to discern the unknown.
4. Righteousness and justice and the problem
of evil and injustice. How do people seek
righteousness and find social order in the
midst of evil and injustice?

Hiebert warns that ministry professionals like
missionaries are not normally prepared to deal
with people with these types of folk religious
beliefs. Often those in ministry, especially
Western missionaries, are concerned for ultimate
realities, while people in folk religion are trying to
cope with everyday life (1984, 222-23).

Much of folk religion in Japan is, not unlike
folk religions of other people, a mix of formal
religious concepts and animistic beliefs rather
than following some great traditions of formal
religion such as Shinto and Buddhism. Shinto is
unorganized; Buddhism has accommodated to
Shinto.

Befu suggests that,

the system of folk beliefs cannot be
meaningfully divided into its Buddhist,

Shintoist, or Taoist components. To be sure, if one were to trace the historical development of present-day folk beliefs, it would be entirely possible to analyze them into their separate components and discover how and when the fusion took place. But as folk beliefs are practiced now, such academic concern as to how much is Buddhist and how much Shinto has no realistic meaning for the people (1971, 100).

The true religion of Japan is folk religion, not organized religion. "It seems that no organized system of faith exists ... and yet it has become deeply rooted in the sentiment of the majority of the Japanese people" (Chizuo 1985, 248-49). Rather than following formal religion the Japanese are more likely follow the little traditions of the local neighborhood shrines, rites and oral traditions of their immediate family or geographical area (Hiebert & Meneses 1995, 216). Folk religion answers spiritual needs such as the longings of the human heart, the relationship with the supernatural, and conditions of man's understanding of purity and proper place (cf. Macfarlane 2007, 175-77).

Hori in his book *Folk Religion in Japan* outlines various elements of Japanese folk religion as "belief in the continuity between man and deity, or easy deification of human beings; coexistence of different religions in one family or even in one person; strong belief in spirits of the dead in connection with ancestor worship as well as with more animistic conceptions of malevolent or benevolent soul activities (1968, 13). Folk religion in Japan emphasizes ancestor worship because it shares this worldview concerning man, death, and spirits.

New Religions and New New Religions
In the 20th century, based on the traditional core religions of Shintoism, Buddhism, and Confucianism, hundreds of New Religions (*shin-shūkyō*) were birthed in Japan (McFarland 1967; Earhart 2014, 228). "In spite of the great variety of their doctrines, new religions share unity of aspiration and worldview significantly different from those of secular society and from the so-called established religions" (Hardacre 1986, 3). By addressing the "concrete worries and concerns in people's daily lives" (Shimazono 2003, 280) these new religions grew rapidly and are "unquestionably the largest and fastest-growing popular movement" (Garon 1986, 273) with an estimated ten to twenty percent of the Japanese population (Prohl 2012, 241).

These New Religions make calculated breaks with previous religious traditions. They are "in contrast to a tendency of the older faiths to be a personal, clerical, academic, and tradition-

written, these new religions have a way of making ordinary people believe that they are concerned about them and their problems individually, and have a technique, and a fellowship, that can help" (Ellwood 2008, 210). New Religions emphasize providing practical solutions for family and emotional problems (Ellwood 2008, 210) and as a result "one hallmark of New Religions is that they made a more direct appeal to individual faith" (Earhart 2004, 189). They are synergistic and extremely adaptive prompting Earhart to conclude that "these religious movements are as much renovation as innovation as much renewed religious traditions as new traditions" (Earhart 2004, 187).

Other New Religions called the New New Religions (*shin shin-shūkyō*) developed in the 1970s and 80s with no direct connections with Japanese religious traditions. Their religious influences were using sources of Buddhism more rare in Japan such as Tibetan or Vajrayana (or esoteric) Buddhism. They were more part of the "New Age" movement. Some of these new religions are *Agonshu* (Agama School), *Mahikari* (True Light) and *Kofuku no Kagaku* (Science of Happiness). Probably the widest known is *Aum Shinrikyo* (Supreme Truth) the group that attacked Tokyo subway stations March 20, 1995. Because of government pressure they were forced to disband, and its name changed to *Aleph* in 2000 and had a split off by *Hikari no Wa* (The Circle of Rainbow Light) in 2007.

Japanese and Secularism

Japan is a country with deep religious traditions but since the Meiji period has undergone tremendous modernization to become a leader of the world's technology. During this time Japan has received significant pressure to become more secularized. Corwin outlines that at "least five world views have played a major role in the history of Japanese through – Shintoism, Buddhism, Confucianism, Western humanism and existentialism" (Corwin 1972, 95). Historically Japan has been influenced by Western secularism which is seen in many parts of society. However, Japanese are not Western secularists. Japanese are not even Eastern secularists.

A widely held thesis in sociology is that societies through modernization and urbanization (even globalization) see a decline in the authority of religion and religious beliefs and values. This results in people being less involved in religious activities and overall religiosity. However by tracking empirical evidence for over 150 years, this secularization thesis is widely disbelieved by current sociologists (see Stark 1999). Modernization has not proven to cause a decline in religious activity - not just for Western

Christian countries but also for folk religion in Asian nations.

Part of the view of the secularization of Japan is a projection of post-modern thinking from the West (Hiebert et al 1993, 16n). The thinking is that as a society develops the interest in religion should wane, especially when the society adopts a more modern approach with accompanied technology. In Japan "religion per se showed no signs of impending extinction." (Shenk 2016, 67).

There is a debate whether or not Japan actually, was or even continues to be, so modern. Some see Japan has having elements of modernization but yet modernism is not pervasive in society. Others believe that Japan has always been "post-modern" (Meeko 2001, 185) or never having become modern, it is more like "pre-modern post-modernism."

Since World War II and the upheaval of Japanese society after the war, the number of people who prefer a religion has declined steadily indicating the incredible secularization of the society (Ross 1980, 313). Lewis, a cultural anthropologist, has studied beliefs and various aspects of Japanese religion with people of various age groups. His conclusion is after the war there was a change in the Japanese view of religion due to the disillusion with Japanese history and society.

Viewing the continual modernization and demographic changes of Japan, Japanese society has not seen a corresponding rapid decline in religious activities. Though the beliefs of Japanese have changed over the generations, the practice of religion statistically has remained basically unchanged (Lewis 2013, 243-44). After the *Aum Shinrikyo* gas attack in 1995, people reporting interest in religion dropped but later the survey numbers who believed in religion rebounded back over 70% (Lewis 2018, 242). Most Japanese continue to be disinclined toward organized religion.

While many Japanese move away from organized religion, they continue to practice folk religion while continuing to insist that they are non-religious. "Only a few actually reject the value of religion or are atheists ... and about 75 percent feel that religious attitude is important (Ama 2004, 1).

The level of religiosity, particularly folk religion and its practice, continues to be strong among Japanese (Lewis 2018, 28-29) and there is increasing interest in divination (Lewis 2018, 123). Some scholars still believe that Japan is steadily becoming secular (see Netland 2015, 68-70), but Mullins feels that Japan has a version of a "secular" society but yet with a "religious spirit" (Mullins 2012, 80).

In spite the facts of an actively practicing ancestor cult in Japan, McGavran considers that secular influences in Japan have undermined the belief system supporting this ancestor worship (McGavran 1985, 309). Secular influence has been a challenge to traditional religion in Japan. Yet, the religion of the common people, folk religion, has been remaking itself over and over.

Conclusion

To understand the soil of Japan, we have probed a bit more on the religious traditions of Shinto, Buddhism, Confucianism, Taoism, and Folk Religion. These five religious traditions continue to change and influence the religious beliefs of Japanese (Earhart 2004, 137). We have examined the New Religions and secularism in brief. In the next chapter we will investigate Japanese religious attitudes and motivation before moving on to Part Two of the book.

6

Japanese Religious Practices and Motivations

While working on this book I received a dazzling magazine. The glossy magazine was from a premier builder of Japanese homes. The company is extremely sizeable with a high reputation and listed on the Tokyo stock exchange. As I paged through the collection of interesting articles on residential architecture, interior design, and home décor, I saw an article that at first stunned me. There in this magazine on fine homes was a one-page exposé on the benefits of palmistry or palm reading (*tesō*). On further reflection I was not surprised as Japanese religious practices are everywhere, even where you least expect them.

The historical and current religious belief system of the Japanese has been outlined along with a framework for comparing this belief system with others, especially the Biblical Worldview.

Japan has many cultural values that define what is good and beneficial behavior. These values have been explained in other books on Japanese culture. Here is just a short list of significant Japanese cultural values.

- Group Consciousness
- Concern for Obligations
- Hierarchical Social Structure
- Honor, dependability and loyalty
- Cleanliness

The influence of worldview, beliefs, and values generates many religious practices and behavior. Many books on Japanese religion contain details of religious practices. Here is a just a broad sampling.

- Rituals – *hatsumode* (New Year's visits), *higan* (grave visit), *setsubun* (spring festival).
- Local Festivals exhibit much diversity
- Rites of passage – birth, 3,5,7 blessings, coming of age, marriage, etc.
- Funerals – a significant rite of passage

But what are the common Japanese religious practices and what are the motivations for these beliefs?

Practicing Beliefs

Are Japanese religious? Looking at the participation in religious activities at Shinto shrines, Buddhist temples, on religious holidays, and involvement at a personal level, Japanese still continue to be very religious. As mentioned in the previous chapter, over 70% of Japanese believe in religion of some kind and live out their beliefs with religious practices.

Lack of belief in a specific religion does not mean a rejection of religious practices or of participation in religious rituals. According to surveys about 60% of the Japanese turn to the gods in time of distress, more than half of the population believe in the existence of a 'soul' after death and about 63% pay attention to lucky and unlucky days. Charms and fortune-telling are popular among about 75% of the population, about 75% of the homes have family altars (*kamidana* or *butsudan*) and over 80% of the population takes part in New Year's visits to Shinto shrines or Buddhist temples.

Modern Japanese are not eager to declare themselves religious when asked, but religion in Japan has always been more a matter of participation in religious rituals than a matter of holding specific beliefs.

Rituals connected with religion, both private and public, are so much everyday events that very few Japanese are not involved in one way or another (Andreasen 1993, 33-34).

The use of *butsudans* is still pervasive in Japan. In rural areas as many as 90% of the homes may have a *butsudan* where in urban areas it may be down to about 60%, but many urban homes are too small for an altar and many urban nuclear families have not yet had a death in the family (Nakamaki 2003, 23-25).

David Lewis has conducted survey research and collected data from other surveys. Table 1 includes data from the Gallop survey conducted in 2001 (Lewis 2018) showing 30-60% of Japanese, especially pre-teens and teenagers, are active in various folk religious practices.

Type of Practice	Adults	Teenagers	Pre-teens	Lewis Page
Mikuji Oracles	57.4	48.9	57.3	116
Mamori Charms	53.7	36.0	50.7	154
'Western' Astrology	21.5	33.4	28.3	119-20

Table 1 - Gallop Poll Data

Other practices are still widespread as 43.1% of women (11.2% of men) have practiced blood group divination (Lewis 2018, 121) and palmistry is practiced by 20-40% of Japanese depending on the age and generation (Lewis 2018, 118).

In many ways Japanese religion is practiced my most Japanese, but some Japanese actually doubt the truths that support it. Some Japanese do not believe in life after death, yet they still partake in the rituals that support the ancestor cult. Some Japanese are secular, and do not believe in a soul that survives death, still they continue practicing their religion (Lewis 2013, 217-18 & 243-44). What is the reason for this discrepancy?

Religious Motivations

The importance of a religious belief system as part of a core worldview forms the basis for religious practices. In order to understand the religious practices, we must take a step back as "an essential first step was to try to understand the kinds of motivations which lay behind existing religious practices in Japan" (Lewis 2001, 11). There are several motivations that have been suggested. Probably for each person their motivation could include a combination of several of these.

First, obligation to others has been suggested. The Japanese constantly live under obligations to others around them, and even the deceased. Their religious practices are continued due to social pressure. This web of social obligations and relationships called *nihonkyō* (Japanism) is being considered as the basis of current Japanese society (see Lundell 1995). Many have mentioned that they continue in Japanese religious practices but without belief due to pressure from family members (Lewis 2013, 145-46).

Second, this fear of breaking obligations to relations is coupled with a fear of spiritual or moral consequences. For some Japanese the "motivation for performing those rites is a fear of supernatural vengeance if they are not performed properly" (Lewis 2013, 239). This could simply be a fear of *bachi* or divine punishment. Some Japanese have great fear of not performing the correct rituals to prevent the *goryō* or vengeful spirits from carrying out their misfortune (*tatari*) on the living. Befu outlines several reasons for misfortune (*tatari*) such as neglecting a god, and taboo (1971, 113). There is also the accompanying fear of spirit possession (*tsuki*) (Befu 1971, 112-13) by the spirits of foxes or dogs (Hori 1968, 45) for not being dutiful in religion.

Third, the motivation for continuing grave rites and ceremonies can be identified as custom, tradition, following the education and customs of the previous generation. Lewis found that two-thirds of those he surveyed visited the grave sites of their family at *obon* or *higan* (Lewis 2018, 268). The motivation for ancestral rites are many including benefiting those who have died, fear of revenge from the dead, thanksgiving, respect for ancestors, and for dealing with memories and feelings for that person (Lewis 2018, 278-80). One man whose wife died in a car accident continues to perform *butsudan* practices because he felt she died in his place and he needs to sooth his guilt for her death (Lewis 2018, 256).

Other general religious motivations are concern for safety, gaining reassurance about a decision, or simply peace of mind and heart. The increasing interest in divination and fortune-telling is a desire, particularly for the young, to assist in making decisions and finding assurance (Lewis 2018, 123). A most prominent use of religion among young people in daily life is related to educational matters, especially the pressure to succeed in school entrance examinations that control much of their futures (Reader 1991, 183).

The human heart is complicated and in the religious realm it becomes even more difficult to determine the basic underlying motivation. One example of the complicated aspects to religion and relationships is part of a case study that David Lewis describes in detail. On the surface one event in Mr. Kinoshita's life, as you can see, was full of convoluted feelings, obligations, longings, and compassion.

When his father's mother became ill with cancer, the whole family went to a shrine

107

specializing in charms and prayers to avert cancer, but the grandmother nevertheless died. Kinoshita-san says that they "did not really believe that my grandmother would recover": their motivations in going to the shrine were ostensibly to appeal to the god for mercy and covertly to "beguile the mind and distract attention" from the illness (Lewis 2018, 319).

For those interested in understanding more deeply the religious motivations of Japanese, I would encourage you to read David Lewis's book *Religion in Japanese Daily Life*. It is full of specific examples and ethnographies of various families.

Belief and Practice

Japanese hesitate to reveal that they really do not believe in what they are practicing. But possibly part of the reason for the above discrepancy is how Japanese actually view their religion. The Japanese view of religion is that which is not necessarily logically true but experientially true. In this sense Japanese are "post-modern" in their thinking. Often research anthropologist Lewis would question people who did not seem to believe in what they were practicing. The standard answer was, "well it cannot hurt," or "it may actually work." To them there was no conflict of belief and practice due to its experiential benefits.

As Japanese religion is often esoteric, Japanese often practice religion without any concern for its meaning. This would explain the use of the word "faith" and "belief" among the Japanese. Faith is more like a subjective feeling rather than a dependence or trust in an outside object or person. This also reveals the apparent need for Japanese to make their religion internal and experientially based.

But from the Biblical point of view, we can also see discrepancies of belief and practice as evidence of a continual search for meaning and belief. There has been a surge in the last few years of "common religion" because of the need to find practical answers to problems related to the long economic slump of Japan, which has undermined the confidence of people in Japan's global leadership (Reader & Tanabe 1998, 42). Japanese are looking for answers regarding their identity, which has given rise to a myriad of new religions or *shin shūkyō* and *shin shin shūkyō* (Hiebert et al 1999, 357-58)

People are religious because man is a worshipping creature and spiritually is a dimension that is true for all people. Paul makes it clear that people worship wrongly because of an expression of real inner spiritual need (Rom 1:18ff). The Japanese continue to reinvent reasons for religious beliefs and practices. This phenomenon may come as a surprise to some sociologists but is not surprising for those with a Christian Worldview who are familiar with the fallen nature of man and his continual efforts to create an object of worship besides the creator God of the Bible.

Here we have surveyed the religious practices and motivations of the Japanese. This ends our exploration of the soil of Japan. In Part One of this book we investigated the nature of Japanese religion, we looked at Japanese religious beliefs both broadly and in detail, we also examined the religious headwaters for Japanese beliefs, and we briefly considered practices and motivations for these beliefs. In Part Two we turn to explore how to share the gospel in this soil of Japan.

Part Two

Sowing the Gospel

7

Understanding Contextualization

In Part One of this book we have attempted to outline the soil of Japan by presenting the religious belief system and its underlying core worldview. We have explored what the Japanese believe to be true and how they see reality, their view of the world.

In Part Two of the book we turn to sowing the gospel in that Japanese soil. We will begin by discussing a very vital topic of. Then through issues related to missiology and theology we will discuss concerns for Christian advance in Japan. We will close this part of the book with some principles and practices for sowing and harvesting in the Japanese soil. This will include practical guidelines in application for those who are on the front lines of ministry.

The Challenge of Japanese Soil

History has taught us through a long line of writers on the subject that contextualizing the gospel message for the Japanese culture is extremely difficult. Getting a grip on the Japanese worldview, understanding the Japanese system of beliefs, and integrating various cultural elements have presented a daunting task in the history of Christian missions. The soil of Japan, its culture, presents one of the greatest missiological challenges. How do we seed or transplant the gospel into the Japanese soil in such a way that the gospel thrives? For over 150 years Protestant workers with much care and competence have seeded and transplanted the gospel in Japan. Many have made sacrifices and dedicated years of service to bringing the gospel to the Japanese. Unfortunately a commensurate result of the gospel taking sufficient root in Japanese soil has not followed. Those currently working among the Japanese should be intensely thankful for those who came before us as we stand on their shoulders.

This brings us to the topic of contextualization, the adapting of mission approaches to produce the result of a dynamic indigenized faith. A thorough discussion of contextualizing the gospel for the Japanese culture is such a massive topic and more suitable for another entire book, so this chapter will present only an overview.

The Necessity of Contextualization

The lack of proper contextualization of the gospel in Japan has been cited as a main reason for a corresponding lack of response of the Japanese people to the gospel. In my other book I list contextualization as one of the three main contributors to the Japanese being identified as an "unreached people group" (Mehn 2017, 7-8). Because this significant problem is a cultural one, we must contextualize (cf. Fukuda 1993, 3). Some feel that the gospel message needs radical adaptation in the Japanese culture. From my observations, many people have a high interest in this topic which needs to be understood conceptually as well as practically. Here I will present a short introduction to contextualization and its related topics.

Contextualization Defined

Contextualization is much more than solely good cross-cultural communication, adjustment and relevance to the culture. Moreau offers us a helpful definition of contextualization as "the process whereby Christians adapt the forms, content and praxis of the Christian faith so as to communicate it to the minds and hearts of people with other cultural backgrounds. The goal is to make the Christian faith *as a whole*—not only the

117

message but also the means of living out of our faith in the local setting—understandable" (Moreau 2005, 323). The goal of contextualization is a vibrant community of disciples of Jesus rooted in the indigenous soil of a people. "If the church is be indigenous it must spring up in the soil from the very first seeds planted" (Allen 1962, 2).

Contextualization is widely accepted and taught in evangelical seminaries and mission schools throughout the world. Contextualization for many decades has been an extremely hot area of discussion and debate in missiological circles. Its origins and beginnings seemed to promote a compromise of the gospel as earlier proponents began with neo-orthodox approaches and liberal theology. These approaches were carefully watched and cautioned by evangelicals. Later some viewed contextualization as some kind of compromise for simply making the gospel relevant. But evangelicals continued to interact with other scholars with the goal of bringing the gospel to cultures in such a way that would transform them. As explained by Keller,

> Contextualization is not - as it is often argued - "giving people what they want to hear." Rather, it is giving people the Bible's answers, which they may not at all want to hear, to questions about life that people in their particular time and place are

asking, in language and forms they can comprehend, and through appeals in arguments with force they can feel, even if they reject them. (Keller 2012, 89).

Over the last thirty years, several models of contextualization have been developed. Most evangelical models have valuable merits and we will look at one extremely valuable model later. A few models have a more radical understanding of contextualization such as "insider movements" among Muslims and Hindus. Without getting into a long description here, most evangelicals have rejected these radical understandings as not appropriate biblical models. But many writers have pointed out, there are many examples in the Bible of contextualization.

Biblical Contextualization

Various writers point to examples in the book of Acts where the apostles and believers endeavored to contextualize the gospel. Especially for us in Japan, insights can be gleaned from the story of Simon the sorcerer (Acts 8:9ff), Paul's approach to the polytheists at Lystra and Derbe (14:6-17), or the urban pluralistic Greeks on the Areopagus in Athens (17:16-34). But like other narrative passages of the Bible, these events should be seen only as descriptive of what happened and not prescriptive for other eras or contexts.

Paul explains his approach to ministry more clearly in didactive sections of scripture such as First Corinthians 9:16–23. Paul shares his sense of priority and the unchangeable nature of the gospel (vv. 16–17). The gospel must be preached for the salvation of all people (v16) and he does not shrink from showing people's need of Christ. Yet Paul also talks about how he adapted himself, not just his message, to the condition of other people (vv. 20-23). For Paul, and us, this means a great sacrifice of relinquishing personal freedom in incarnating the gospel and adapting our ministry approaches. Paul in his desire to "to win as many as possible" (v. 19) goes to great lengths in contextualizing. "I have become *all* things to *all* people so that by *all* possible means" [emphasis added] (v. 22). Paul was flexible in order to make the gospel central in his ministry, not to erect barriers to understanding, or present the gospel of Jesus as something alien and incomprehensible.

The New Testament has many examples of contextualization. Dean Flemming in his volume *Contextualizing in the New Testament: Patterns for Theology and Mission* surveys the entire New Testament for examples and patterns of contextualization (Flemming 2005). He surveys many topics that include preaching, cultural engagement, doing theology, and syncretism. His biblical theology approach includes the Book of

Acts and the writings and ministry of Paul along with the gospels and the Book of Revelation.

A Theological View of Culture

Culture is a creation of man from the patterns of his society. For each member of a society the culture determines: what is real, what is true, what is good, and what should be done. Man develops culture from the world around him. This is the world that God created and sustains and into which he has revealed himself.

Romans teaches that God has revealed himself in nature sometimes identified as "common grace" or general revelation. Romans 1:19-20 affirms, "because that which is known about God is evident within them; for God made it evident to them. For since the creation of the world His invisible attributes, His eternal power and divine nature, have been clearly seen, being understood through what has been made, so that they are without excuse" (NASB). Every man and woman already knows they are to glorify and thank God as the true God, but everyone resists God (v. 21). general revelation does not reveal a saving knowledge of God (Rom 10:14), but through it the creator speaks to man about his existence and sovereign rule so that man has no excuse for not worshiping the true God.

Every culture has the exposure of general revelation but also every culture shares in the fallenness of man. Man's fallenness affects all

121

aspects of man including truth perception, the knowledge of God, man's focus of worship, and even social relationships. Paul in Romans chapter one reveals a downward spiral (v. 18) of depravity - caused by man's rebellion against the sovereign creator God - that affects all man's perceptions (v. 21).

Due to man's wickedness, the truth is then suppressed, that leads to hearts darkened, and minds left to depravity (v. 28). In Romans, Paul declares that the biblical God has clearly revealed himself in nature as an almighty creator (vv. 19, 20). But man in his fallen sinful state has exchanged God's glory for images and they worshipped "created things rather than the creator" (v. 25). This sin of man is both individual and corporate in its nature. This described human rebellion against God becomes manifested in human systems that do not glorify God but rebel against him. Widespread worship of idols throughout Japan is an obvious and contemporary example of Paul's teaching here in Romans.

Because of the ongoing role of general revelation speaking to men's hearts and the continuing condition of man's fallenness and rebellion generating depravity, there is a constant dynamic of God's truth continually being proclaimed (v. 20) and men actively suppressing the truth (v. 19). As a result every "human culture is an extremely complex mixture of brilliant truth, marred half-truths, and overt resistance to the truth" (Keller 2014, 109). So cultures should be celebrated but we must also have a great suspicion about them. The Lausanne Covenant asserts that, "Culture must always be tested and judged by Scripture. Because men and women are God's creatures, some of their culture is rich in beauty and goodness. Because they are fallen, all of it is tainted with sin and some of it is demonic" (Lausanne Covenant #10).

As man is fallen, we must consider that in every culture there are corporate and cultural sins as well as individual transgressions. Christians too are fallen creatures and in spite of our salvation and awareness of special revelation we are not immune to our own errors in determining the truth. All of us are members of human culture and we must understand culture in light of general revelation, the image of God in man, the fall, as well as the transforming power of the gospel.

Key Essentials in Contextualization
In approaching a culture we must be very sensitive to our sources of truth, means of knowledge (epistemology) but ultimately our concern should be for the authority of scripture. This authority of God's holy word is both challenging and personal to us.

An Ultimate Commitment to Scripture

There is absolute truth. As Christians our authority for truth comes from the scriptures. Contextualization demands seeing the cultural context with theological lenses. As we have already said, Christian responses for the Japanese beliefs and worldview may require review and possible re-emphasis of several theological areas, while other responses will require development specifically for the Japanese context. Each of us come to the Bible from our own cultural perspective and we can personally gravitate to our preferred sections or teachings of scripture. Believing in the prime authority of the Bible, we must engage the culture of Japan as a basis for viewing the scriptures with fresh eyes. This freshness will, with the help of the Holy Spirit, enable us to learn and discover new perspectives that include new cultural categories in application for the Japanese. Typical Western theological training is not designed to address every cultural issue generated by Japanese religious beliefs (see next chapter). As people desirous of indigenous Japanese churches we must allow the universal absolute truths of scripture to challenge us as Christ's disciples and servants.[8]

---

[8] Contextualizing, seen by some, is involved in "theologizing" in the indigenous culture. Theologies founded in Japanese experience have been developed by

Respectful Commitment to Context

One error in contextualization would be to begin solely with the context. This allows the context to set the agenda rather than the authoritative Word of God. Though context is in a secondary role to scripture, "we must be equally careful not to minimize the role of context" (Ott & Strauss 2010, 278). As we are called by God to love and serve the Japanese people, we must be sympathetic and respectful towards their entire culture including their beliefs and worldview. We need to present to Japanese a Christ which is neither foreign nor alien. Our communication should be clear to their hearts and minds. We should be flexible, be as winsome as possible under gospel authority, and connect to people's inner hopes and dreams as exemplified by Paul.

Culture is manmade and by nature affected by the fall of man, so every culture has elements that are opposed to the Trinitarian God and the Christian Worldview. But on the other hand, due to general revelation and the image of God in man, every culture also has some elements that more easily harmonize with Christian truth. The

Kanzo Uchimura, Kazoh Kitamori, Toyohiko Kagawa, Kosuke Koyama, Shushaku Endo, and others. This topic is too complex to sufficiently discuss in this book. For more investigation please study J. Nelson Jennings's article on "Japanese Theology" (2003) or, for a longer treatment, not from an evangelical perspective, Yasuo Furuya's A History of Japanese Theology (1997).

difficulty in contextualizing is not just making adjustments and adaptions in the receiving culture but also discerning what elements are helpful and harmful for that process. Contextualization is a skill that involves much discernment, balance, and focus.

> The great missionary task is to express the gospel message to a new culture in a way that avoids making the message unnecessarily alien to that culture, yet without removing or obscuring the scandal in the offense of biblical truth. A contextualize gospel is marked by clarity and attractiveness, and yet it still challenges sinners' self-sufficiency and calls them to repentance. It adapts and connects to the culture, yet at the same time challenges and confronts it (Keller 2012, 89)

Models of Contextualization

Evangelical missiologists have dialogued over the subject of contextualization since it was introduced as a topic in missiology over thirty years ago. Over that time, many theological issues and concerns have been voiced and proponents have differed over methodologies and praxis. As a result, many evangelical models of contextualization have been presented.[9]

One of the most insightful models has been expounded by mission anthropologist Paul Hiebert. Many writers have found his Critical Contextualization model extremely valuable and it is one of most widely referenced model in contextualization (Hiebert 1984).

Hiebert's Critical Contextualization

What Hiebert means in the use of the adjective "critical" was not that contextualization in itself was dangerous or that we need to be overly fault-finding. As issues in contextualization are of a vital importance, we have to take great care in discerning what should be permissible because every culture contains both good and evil. "Rather than thoughtlessly rejecting all old cultural practices or uncritically accepting them, they should undergo a process of critical contextualization" (Ott & Strauss 2010, 281–82). In short, our arrival at a diagnosis and treatment must be conducted with careful thought and application.

For workers in a cross-cultural setting, "the question is not *whether* they will contextualize, but *how well* they will contextualize (Moreau

---

[9] For a fuller discussion of evangelical models of contextualization please see A. Scott Moreau's *Contextualization in World Missions: Mapping and Assessing Evangelical Models* 2012. Grand Rapids, MI: Kregel Academic.

2018, 230). When a cross-cultural worker reflects on the practices of the old culture he is working there are several possible responses that can be made (See figure 13). One response is that we can reject the old ways because we believe the old culture is only evil. This denial of the old culture results in no contextualization for that culture at all. A second response is to accept all of the old ways, that the old culture is all good, and we adopt uncritical contextualization. Both of these responses seem like easy and "quick fixes" to the challenge of indigenizing Christian faith in a culture.

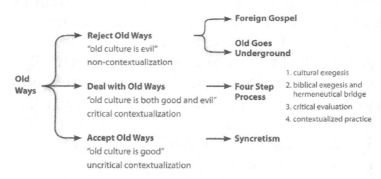

Figure 13 Adapted from Hiebert & Meneses, In Ott & Strauss 282

But a third way of dealing with the old ways is by seeing the old culture as having both good and evil elements. Hiebert's critical contextualization shows the necessary four step process of trying to discern what should be done, which is developed further below. Contextualization should not be assumed to be an easy process.

Non-contextualization

Rejecting the old culture as evil means there is no attempt to adjust or indigenize Christian faith; there is no contextualization. One result is that the old beliefs continue to be practiced but they may be practiced in secret and develop and underground movement of the old practices. This leads to syncretism - a mixture of faith systems - or develops into a kind of dual religion or split-level Christianity, which is disconnected public and private religion.

One example, seen by many scholars (Jennings 2003, 184; Miyazaki 2003, 22, 31; Furuya 2006, 42-45), is the *Kakure Kirishitan* or hidden Christians who practiced their version of Christianity in secret due the systematic persecution during the Edo Period (1603-1868). Their beliefs and practices were an intermingling of Christian, Buddhism, Japanese folk religion, and Mariolatry. When the government persecution ended, they renounced their secrecy and they wished to reenter the Roman Catholic church, their historical origin. They were not welcomed back into the Catholic church due to their heretical beliefs and practices.

Besides going underground another result of non-contextualization is the gospel is viewed as something foreign. Many Japanese view Christianity as foreign and not an indigenous religion. Incarnating the gospel in Japanese soil should result in a flourishing indigenous church. In the history of Japan the development of religious belief systems is predominately stories of adaptions of other foreign religions (Mullins 2006, 115).

> As a relatively late-arrival, Christianity has perhaps had more difficulty in shedding its 'foreign' images and associations than has Buddhism and hence has remained a minority religion throughout its history in Japan" (Mullins 2006, 118).

Numerous researchers of Christianity and the culture of Japan has focused on this problem. The overall conclusion is the same, in sharp contrast to a healthy tree being rooted in Japanese soil. Many have concluded the church resembles a bonsai tree (Corwin 1978) or a "potted plant" (Conn 1984, 246) that both have restricted growth due to their bound roots not having healthy growth of other trees flourishing freely in unlimited soil.

Christianity in Japan continues to try to shake off the stigma of foreignness. Robert Lee's conclusion of his research on the Japanese church in the 1960s was that the gospel was a "" and viewed as alien and foreign (Lee 1967, 163). "The church in Japan still does not relate well to the Japanese society, and it has difficulty in communicating to the people in a meaningful way" (Solheim 1984, 213). To reach Japanese culture and society, this reality has directed some leaders to consider some significant changes through contextualization. One key Japanese church leader has asserted, "My evaluation is that Japanese churches have largely failed to become Japanese in order to win the Japanese" (Fukuda 2015, 525). Many like Ralph Winter contend this perspective continues today, asserting "there is not yet a truly Japanese church movement but only a relatively small Westernized following" (Winter 2002, 8).

Several Japanese pastors were discussing the days of the post-war development of many of the denominations that now exist. They felt that probably the right decisions were made about the culture but sometimes the old Japanese culture was just completely rejected out of hand without careful discernment and consideration. Many concurred that that discernment should have been applied better. During that time Christianity was viewed more favorably by Japanese due to the post–war occupation. Many of these leaders shared regret about those days because it is difficult to go back and undo those decisions. I thought it was very interesting that none of these Japanese church leaders mentioned any particular cultural practice or element that they were concerned about changing. Their sense was more of a broader understanding of the Japanese culture that was rejected by the church. The immediate post-war period included a desire to be different from the Japanese culture and the church seemed caught up in that wave.

One hinderance to Christianity becoming indigenous is Japan's own perception of itself. Religion among the Japanese and the nation of Japan has an intimate connection. Many Japanese do not realize that much of their religious tradition was borrowed from Buddhism and religions from China (see chapter 5). Shinto and Buddhism have a long history of traditions and both were official religions of Japan at one time. The national identity of the Japanese (*nihonkyō*) is intertwined with these religious systems. A sense of national identity and religious character has been propelled by former State Shintoism and its tremendous influence through (*tennōsei*) the emperor system (Lee 1995, 118–23). "All of this added up to an ethnocentricity whereby the Japanese viewed themselves as the children of the gods, possessing a culture superior to any other" (Mathiesen 2006, 99). Part of the source for this movement was cultural nationalism in pre-war

Japan and a continuing viewpoint of cultural uniqueness (*nihonjinron*) in post-war Japan (Sugimoto 2014, 16–24). These are often debated topics, but what is often understood by typical Japanese is that they are Japanese and therefore followers of Shinto and Buddhist traditions whereas Christianity is a foreign religion and not Japanese.

We ministry workers, both Japanese and expatriate, as people who desire to see Japanese believe in the gospel, must make all efforts to contextualize the gospel. We have to speak in Japanese with religious terminology that people can understand. We really cannot avoid contextualization as we either do it well or we do it poorly. Everything we do is laden with culture, often our own, so we must do our best to contextualize consciously and with intention.

Uncritical Contextualization

Uncritical Contextualization begins with the determination that the old culture is good. There is great danger in just adapting any Japanese cultural element without a deep understanding of the culture. This problem is particularly dangerous when well-meaning workers attempt using cultural elements on their own without significant help from those culturally aware of Japan. This author is aware of some of the complexities of the Japanese religious culture and many individual's ideas on what we should adapt from the Japanese culture. However, I am extremely hesitant to offer hints or suggestions in this book, because I feel more investigation is warranted and many more experienced individuals need to be involved. To me these are potentially very dangerous places to explore on your own without adequate preparation.

> We must deeply respect other cultures. However, an uncritical acceptance of them, like an uncritical acceptance of our own culture, devalues the transforming power of the gospel (Hiebert & Meneses 1995, 168).

In contextualizing some element out of hand, there is a great danger of making the gospel captive to cultures if they are not seen as fallen and sinful. Moving in the direction of uncritical contextualization without adequate discernment means entering the dangerous road to syncretism.

The Danger of Syncretism

In Hiebert's diagram there are two routes leading to syncretism. One is *non-contextualizing* where the old religion goes underground and compromises with Christianity. The other way is the belief that the old culture is not evil and *uncritically contextualizing* the Christian faith, leading to compromise. Both of these routes end up at syncretism.

In indigenizing or adapting the gospel into a culture, the gospel may be compromised. Syncretism happens when the full authority of the Bible is not applied in determining truth in other cultures. We do not have the freedom to pick and choose between beliefs, rather we must be consistent with biblical truth. Learning from Paul in 1 Corinthians 9, God's absolute truth must remain the priority in adapting the gospel, or the gospel may lose its prophetic power to speak to a culture. "Syncretism occurs when the purity of the Gospel message or the essential functions of the church are sacrificed at the altar of relevance" (Ott & Wilson 2011, 124). As shared earlier, Japanese are quick to adopt religious ideas and include beneficial ones in their belief systems. We must remember that Christianity is a religion of exclusive belief in Jesus Christ as the only Savior and that this gospel can be an offense to unbelievers.

Even today Christian workers are tempted to simply compromise with the culture and therefore enter the road of syncretism leading to false doctrine and even heresy. We are amply warned by Japanese religious history which contains many examples of the compromise of syncretism and false teaching such as the *Kakure Kirishitan* or hidden Christians mentioned earlier, and it seems a majority of the examples of indigenous movements outlined in Mullins book *Christianity Made in Japan.*

Critical Contextualization for Japan

How can the Japanese culture be penetrated by the gospel so that the gospel flourishes in the soil of Japan? How can the community of faith, the church, be deeply embedded in Japanese soil? Critical contextualization exegetes both the Bible and the culture as "good contextualization draws on scripture as its primary source but recognizes the significant role that context will play in shaping theology and practice" (Ott & Strauss 2010, 283–84). Critical contextualization deals with the old culture viewing it as having both evil and good elements. Hiebert suggests a four-step process in doing critical contextualization.

1. Exegete the Culture

In critical contextualization the first step is cultural exegesis or understanding the full meaning in adaptations in that culture. But we do not start with the culture as the authority, for the scripture is our supreme authority.

Elements of Japanese culture are sometimes hard to confirm with the Japanese themselves. Due to the value of social reserve, Japanese seem to be reticent to speak to people they do not know well about their cultural views, especially regarding religion. For the writing of this book I discussed Japanese religious beliefs with many Japanese pastors and church leaders. A few of them admitted to me that they were not as familiar with Japanese religious as they had hoped. Also globalization is a reality for all Japanese and makes our contextualization more of a challenge (Ott 2015).

But we gather information about the culture. Gospel sowers need two-way listening and reflecting, engaging, and responding with the culture (Ott & Strauss 2010, 283–84). This author feels that much more street-level investigation is necessary. Regarding ministry in Japan there are many theoretical and academic books but very little field research and of the case study type that can aid in our investigations.

2. Exegete the Scriptures

Second is the exegesis of the scriptures in which we try to understand what they teach about a particular subject. We need to broadly study biblical teachings about a cultural belief, value, or practice. This involves systematic theology, biblical theology, textual exegesis, and hermeneutics to undercover bridges to another culture.

3. Evaluate Critically

Third is a critical evaluation of the culture where a group of believers make a decision about the old practices. The culture is evaluated with the theological lenses of scripture. As mentioned above, several areas of Japanese culture still need to be further understood, and subsequent contextualization needs to be applied, especially in a rapidly changing society.

4. Practice Contextualization

Fourthly we contextualize a new Christian practice by implementation. Only after the first three processes are completed do we begin adapting in a new context. Working in theology is hard work, but that is not where the process ends. The process is also in applying that theology in practice and making sure the theology is worked out in reality.

In critical contextualization, workers must choose what to do with cultural elements, there are many possible responses (Ott & Strauss 2010, 281–83).

1. Adoption - The cultural practice does not violate the Bible and can be retained.
2. Rejection - The cultural practice is seen as violating biblical theology and is rejected.
3. Modification - A new Christian meaning can be given to a previous practice.

4. Substitution - An alternative Christian practice can replace one in the culture.

5. - A practice may not be a biblical ideal but promoting change immediately in this practice may cause more harm considering other biblical teachings. Often there is a transition period where a final solution is worked out over time.

The practice of contextualizing missions has always been more than theoretical theology. Mission is an iterative or repetitive process where the community of faith examines the scriptures to determine how to faithfully communicate the gospel in every area of the receiving culture. After careful formulation, a course of action is determined. Once these adaptations have been applied the theology is again reviewed and checked. More adjustment in practice maybe warranted. So it becomes an endless spiral of theory and practice where ministry application informs mission theology and then theology determines practice.

Contextualization, because of its scope and complexity, should not be done by individuals working alone. "Contextualization that connects will always be done in community" (Ott & Strauss 2010, 284). Throughout history a community of faith engaged in ministry while they examined the Word of God.

> Professional theologians can play a key role as facilitators and guides in the process of contextualization, but the entire body of believers should be part of the process (Ott & Strauss 2010, 284).

Conclusion

The gospel in Japanese soil presents a daunting task in contextualizing the gospel.

> The Japanese identification with gods in nature, the importance of the family, the significance of specific rituals and amulets, the prominence of individual cults—these all integrate religious activities into everyday life (Earhart 2014, 15).

As was shared in chapter one, Japanese religion is often unstructured, defies analysis, adapts by making use of many elements, and is intensely practical. Though the Japanese continue to follow many religious themes, the religious scene in Japan is gradually changing. Each of these themes continue to drive Japanese behavior and practice making communicating the gospel to the minds and hearts of Japanese extremely challenging and demands both holistic and rigorous commitment by all Christians.

> By rooting all theology and practice in scripture, penetrating to the level of

worldview, and interacting with every aspect of context, we can help ensure the emergence of healthy churches that connect with and transform their worlds (Ott & Strauss 2010, 290).

Understanding the process of contextualization leads us to the overall goal of a flourishing indigenous church among the Japanese.

In this chapter we overviewed the concept and application of contextualization. Several other missiological and theological issues that impinge on the Christian advance in Japan will be outlined in the next chapter.

8

Towards Christian Advance in Japan

I was training a group of missionaries on Japanese belief systems. To begin, I had mentioned common Japanese practices like numerology, divination, and fortune-telling. One of the church planting pastors said, "Well that is just because Japanese are superstitious." Another church planter said he just ran into a young person currently attending his church who was on the way to the Buddhist temple because he had to deal with his *kegare* (impurity). But he said that generally he was doubtful whether the people he was evangelizing practiced other folk religious beliefs. So I asked that pastor if the young people they are trying to reach for the gospel follow astrology? He thought and then affirmed that they do. And I then asked him about some other common practices among Japanese, and again he admitted that they did them as well. So in one seminar we had one pastor who views Japanese religious beliefs as superstitions and another pastor who is somewhat unconscious that the people he's trying to reach are actively involved in these religious practices.

Take Japanese Beliefs Seriously

We must take the belief systems of the Japanese seriously if we intend to address the gospel to Japanese people. Authors describing Japanese cultural elements often focus on religion at the phenomenological level, meaning what ways do Japanese practice religion and how do you describe their experience. These writers focus mainly on the actual religious behavior and do not often consider the belief systems that underlie those religious practices. As a result, much of what is written about Japanese religion is cataloging religious forms and rites. If we reconsider Kwast's diagram from the introduction, the focus is mainly on what is done (possibly values), however, the focus is not on what is true and what is real to the Japanese. To understand and transform a culture we must move beyond practices and values to affect the worldview which is at the core. If we do not address the culture at the worldview level, we face the dangers of syncretism (Hesselgrave 2006, 71).

A typical response to Japanese religious practices is simply attributing all of Japanese beliefs to superstition and failing to understand their meaning. Taylor observed missionary responses and determined that a "great frustration of missionaries in this country is the continued existence in modern Japan of what Westerners think of as a 'primitive,' preindustrial religious mentality" (1983, 138). Hiebert agrees that given, "our Western view of things, we do not take folk religion seriously. Consequently, we do not provide biblical answers to the everyday questions the people face" (1984, 223). If we truly want to address the heart needs of people, we will take Japanese religion and their beliefs seriously. We do not have to agree with their beliefs, and we should not as they contain theological error. However, to the Japanese these beliefs define reality and make sense. They cannot be written off as mere superstition. In our cultural engagement we must confront them with the Christian Worldview of the living God.

For new missionaries, pastors, and believers our effectiveness in impacting the culture is in direct proportion to the amount of understanding that we have of the average Japanese and our ability to relate the gospel to those beliefs. At times there seems to be a deep lack of awareness of this vital feature of the Japanese culture. As pointed out by a Japan scholar raised in a missionary home, "One of the reasons that the Christian churches have failed to make much headway in Japanese society is their failure to take seriously the 'common religion of Japan'" (Mullins 1998, 239n13).

Engage the Culture Respectfully

We must skillfully observe and listen to the average person. When a Japanese says, "I went to a palm reader because I would like to get married" we need to listen past their behaviors and discern their heart needs and gain insight into their beliefs and worldview. We need to make inquiries, study, and reflect on what we witness and hear.

Connect with the Japanese

Generally formal religion answers questions about personal beliefs that Japanese are often not considering. Indeed a few Japanese become Christians by contemplating their ultimate origin, purpose, and destiny (Hiebert et al 1999, 74ff). However, Japanese tend to be more concrete in their thought processes, rather than pondering some deep philosophies. Most Japanese grapple with daily life questions. We need to meet Japanese in their daily life and make faith contact points where they live.

For young people moving toward adulthood, school entrance examinations are periods of intense spiritual interest. Many Christians came to faith in their teen years. Reader did a survey of his students and found 61% pray for the examinations, 33% write an *ema,* and 75% bought a *mamori* (Reader 1991, 183). Connecting with these young people and their entire families can be strategic for evangelism.

Do More Street Level Research

We need to understand Japanese and the basis of their religious beliefs. To get those answers means doing "research" one-on-one and up close. This kind of research is not conducted in books, searches on the internet, collecting a few anecdotes, or interacting with ministry colleagues but talking to typical Japanese where they live, work, and play.

David Lewis' book, *The Unseen Face of Japan,* contains extensive field research which has been well received by mission practitioners in Japan. The real benefits of his later book *Religion in Japanese Daily Life* are the field case studies including actual people, interviews, and situations which give insights into entire families. In reading his book, I felt like Lewis was introducing me to several Japanese families assisting me to understand them in a deep way and the life formation of their religious beliefs

147

and practices. There are other writers like David Ronan who have researched the Japanese act of conversion in relationship to idol and ancestor worship. This type of research of average people needs to be multiplied. Like the work of Lewis and Ronan, more deliberate field research needs to be done by trained practitioners guided and mentored by specialists in mission anthropology and sociology.

The Japanese are not readily going to help this happen. As stated before, Japanese are generally unaware of the nature of their beliefs and they are not used to articulating the logic or coherence of their belief system. If you interview a Japanese on the street asking if they are religious probably most would be evasive. We must be more insightful and find out what personal beliefs they hold. Apart from an anonymous survey, many Japanese will not admit any of their true beliefs.

Determine and Address Felt Needs

Like all human beings Japanese have many felt needs. Many are seeking happiness, self-fulfillment, belonging, and freedom. Only by relating with Japanese as friends can we determine their felt needs.

Many Japanese often come to Christ through crises such as a serious illness, an accident, a loss of a job, or a perceived failure. These crises could have happened to them or a close family member.

These are also times when they seek out religious answers among their Japanese traditions. Andreasen reports that 60% of Japanese turn to religion in time of distress (Andreasen 1993, 33). These crises points are times to determine and address their felt needs (Dyer 2013, 127ff; Fukuda 1993, 183-87).

Provide Solid Christian Answers

What is the gospel? What is good news for the Japanese? "So an important issue is to find out how the gospel can relate to the core of the Japanese culture" (Solheim 1984, 213). We should not accept simplistic answers or mere proof texting but "doing theology" with the Japanese context in mind. This involves solid exegesis, theology and biblical theology. We need to read both the Scriptures and materials on Japanese beliefs. We need to be able to discuss with Japanese their ghost stories, prayer beads, and other religious practices. They need to hear from us another worldview that addresses their underlying needs. The Scriptures encompass a wealth of answers for life's questions. These answers should be provided in humility, by listening to the whole church, seeking Japanese believers for their insight, and taking care to avoid error.

Addressing Japanese Divination

As an example, here is a brief summary of issues to help Japanese in life decisions to seek the creator God rather than divination.

How do people determine life decisions? And especially how are important life decisions made: like what university to attend, what vocation and job to accept, where to live, who to marry, and when to retire? Like most people, Japanese would discuss these matters with their parents, friends, other relatives and their spouse, possibly a professional.

But what if Japanese needed a stronger spiritual power to help them in a really important decision. In a crisis or a major decision many Japanese seek guidance from unseen supernatural forces or powers. To seek guidance, around half of Japanese buy an oracle (*mikuji*) at a temple and nearly a third turn to astrology (*senseijitsu*). Still other Japanese even at the local shopping center may turn to palmistry (*tesō*) or fortune-telling (*uranai*). Young people are attracted to *kokkuri-san*, kind of a Japanese ouiji board, with their friends. There are many other means of divination in Japan like *mamori* charms and in determining to give their child a propitious name many parents resort to *seimei handan*. These are just a few of the many means of divination in Japan.

Everyone needs guidance and direction in life. In answering the need to personal guidance, Christians need to be faithful in modeling and proclaiming the reign of the sovereign God and his overwhelming personal care of our lives. The Bible contains many passages that reveal God's guidance for people. One example is, "I will instruct you and teach you in the way which you should go; I will counsel you with My eye upon you" (Psalm 32:8). King David is saying the creator and sovereign God of the universe provides personal and caring guidance for his children. Notice that David says that God's guidance is in a very personal relationship as he instructs us and teaches us the way. God's guidance is full of his love and care for us (cf. v.10). God promises "I will counsel you and watch over you." Here are promises of great personal security as the creator and sovereign God of the universe provides personal and caring guidance for his children.

Develop Balanced Missional Theology

The Japanese context and its belief systems present several missiological concerns. In order to fully understand Japanese religious beliefs we must understand them from a theological and missiological perspective. As a North American missionary serving in Japan, I have observed several areas needing theological reflection. Each of these challenging themes demand well-balanced, intelligent, scholarly, and practical answers to Japanese religious issues. For many of these issues some missiological theology has already been initiated but much more work is needed.

Develop Theology in Several Areas

1. Theology emphasizing the immanent nature of God while balancing with his transcendent nature.

    Japanese emphasize the closeness or immanence of the gods (*kami*), nature, and human beings from Shinto traditional beliefs. We need to emphasize the transcendent nature of Christian religion, as God as creator and Sovereign, as well as his immanence (Isa 57:14). We need to call attention to both God's divine providence and his personal provision (Acts 17:24–31). For example, when God is called "Our Heavenly Father" those words should resound in our hearts with pregnant meaning. Indeed God is heavenly, holy, and very unlike man; he is transcendent. Simultaneously. he is "Our Father" a very intimate relationship speaking of his immanence.

2. A theology of the sovereignty and love of God over and against fate and Karma.

Many Japanese see their lives controlled by blind luck and much "can't be helped." A Christian Worldview of life is not determined by impersonal destiny but by a loving God's providence and sovereignty. This loving God is in control and he acts in history.

3. A theology of suffering and misfortune.

Why do bad things happen? Pain and suffering are not illusions, as promoted by Buddhism, but they are very real. The Christian understanding of history includes a perfect creation, the fall of man and all nature, full redemption through Christ and his cross and a future renewal. This renewal will be a place with no tears, pain, or death (Rev 7:17), and a new heavens and earth (Rev 21:4,5). A theology of suffering and misfortune must include a solid explanation of the problem of evil (theodicy).

We must answer why there are so many public disasters and suffering as well as the many difficult personal struggles individuals endure. God's reasons for permitting these is not always known but we know that Jesus suffered painfully so that in the future all pain would be removed.

When Japanese struggle with fears of misfortunes such as illness even death sometimes the Christian response is not in the corresponding depths for those issues. Our answers may not be well thought out nor are they effective. "Missionary theology and practice provide little or no solace to Japanese Christians who are troubled by such fears. This is clearly an important dimension of pastoral care in the Japanese context, but something one will not find seriously addressed in the practical theology curriculum of any Protestant seminary in Japan" (Mullins 1998, 153). Christians should be trained to address these issues in the local churches. We need to convey to the Japanese that we worship the God of all comfort, which is our source to comfort others. This is the result of our intimate walk with Christ who experienced sufferings for us (2 Cor 1:3–7).

4. A theology of death and the departed.

Christians need to provide answers to Japanese about death and the loss of their loved ones. These answers must go beyond traditional theology textbooks on personal eschatology. Scripture teaches that "man is destined to die once, and after that to face judgment" (Heb 9:27). We believe those who have died cannot return from the dead. As there is no communication between the dead and the living, therefore the Bible prohibits necromancy or communicating with the dead.

The subject of ancestor worship or ancestor veneration its central to Japanese religion. Much missions research has been done to understand these beliefs and to find suitable Christian adaptations to ancestor rites (see Bong Rin Ro 1985 ed.; Mullins 1998, 144ff; Heisswolf 2018, 180–203). But have the Japanese beliefs lying beneath the ancestor rites been sufficiently addressed? Many have called for more and better Christian responses to the Japanese focus on its ancestors (Hiebert et al 1999, 130-31).

> "In societies with ancestor rights, the church needs to formulate a theology of ancestors. This should make explicit the similarities and differences between Christian and traditional beliefs on such matters as the nature of life after death, the relationship between the ancestors and God, the relationship between the living and the dead, and the connection between the parents and children. It should also deal with the widespread fear that those who die untimely deaths through murders, suicide, or accident become ghosts that plague the living. The church needs to respond sensitively to the question many ask: "Will I join my ancestors if I become a Christian?' (Hiebert & Meneses 1995, 175).

This type of theological work is not just for missionaries but also for the entire church. Japanese would do the best primary theological work in this area as they are suited to understand Japanese culture and will be able to deal with the "excluded middle" better than some Westerners. This contextualization process should be carefully designed and reviewed for Japanese religious belief systems.

5. A theology of the invisible world of powers, authorities, demons, and angels (see below).

6. A theology of divine guidance over against divination.

God intended that he would guide us personally through his word and Spirit rather than mechanistic means such as divination and fortune-telling. God who is personal cares especially for his covenant children (see above).

7. A theology of man in his relationship to nature (the creation) and to the creator.

The Japanese have a deep personal sense of nature. What is man's relationship to God the creator and his creation? What is the nature of man's role as stewards in relationship to nature?

Areas to Develop Balanced Theology

From my perspective, there are several areas that have generated concern about theological balance and the need for caution or warning. In this book we have already met with some cautions. Hiebert has warned us about the issues related to the excluded middle. In the last chapter, we have discussed syncretism and split-level Christianity. This section will introduce four other areas of concern for a more well-rounded theology.

1. Making Religion Practical

Japanese often view Christianity as a religion steeped in education and only interesting for intellectual elites. Christianity in Japan has been accused of being *ronripoi* or "too logical." For many Japanese the way that their religion seems "logical" is that it is practically meeting their needs.

In Reader and Tanabe's book, *Practically Religious: Worldly Benefits and the Common Religion of Japan, the authors* contend that a core aspect of Japanese religion is *genze riyaku*, which means "this-worldly benefits" or "practical benefits in this lifetime." These practical benefits of religion are "primarily material or physical gains such as good health, healing, success, or . . . personal advancement in one's life path, . . . personal well-being and freedom from problems" (Reader & Tanabe 1998, 2). In engaging and contextualizing the gospel for the Japanese, we do not dare abandon the rigorous intellectual foundation of our beliefs revealed by the truth of scripture. But at the same time, we abhor dead orthodoxy, and we lament an absence of full-hearted faith.

We believe that the gospel is relevant and practical for all social and personal needs. But we also resist the promotion of a prosperity gospel where the gospel is watered down to a promise of a better life of health, wealth, and happiness. With the distortion of the prosperity gospel Christian conversion is seen as another line of consumer decisions that benefits the hearers. This is in sharp contrast to the biblical teaching that a believer's life is often marked by pain, suffering, persecution, and even martyrdom. This experience is certainly the facts of history for many Christians in Japan. "Practical experiential religion emanating from a lifestyle of Christian discipleship, obedience of the truth, and missional engagement must be persistently demonstrated in the Japanese context" (Mehn 2017, 16). We must present discipleship with all its costs and at the same time showing that following Jesus is a joyful and fulfilling life (John 7:37-39).

2. Shame and Guilt as Theological Concepts

Since Ruth Benedict published *Chrysanthemum and Sword* in 1946 Japan has been popularly identified as a shame society. In a group conscious society like Japan, your behavior can stain the reputation of your entire group, and you can "lose face" in front of your peers. In many ways, this consciousness and fear of shame can be shown to be the direct reason for many of Japan's social problems like bullying, suicide, hikikomori, and emotional breakdowns.

In some sense, Christianity has not often presented the Christian faith as one that assists people when they feel out of harmony with their peers. This external or shame dimension is also seen in the theological understanding of the relationship between God and man. Throughout the Bible man is identified as one who is shamed as he does not conform to the standards and person of God (cf. Gen 3:7-8).

Studies have shown that Japan is not just a shame society and one dimensional. Japan is also a society where guilt is a real emotion and motivator of people. Motivations of internal guilt and external shame are both valid categories. Lewis has conducted research that show Japanese are widely motivated by guilt (Lewis 2018, 301-4). To take one example, the concept of shame does not sufficiently explain the thousands of statues at temples left by mothers after an abortion. In actuality, shame would in some sense prevent them from acknowledging an abortion. Guilt can explain the need for forgiveness for themselves and for the aborted baby.

Japan continues to be a society where both shame as an external motivator and guilt as an internal motivator are strong inner drives. While some may be delighted to discover the theological understanding of shame as part of the fall of man, we do not want to neglect the forensic guilt of man as well and our need for redemption and forgiveness. Both shame and guilt before God should be used in explaining beliefs to Japanese in our evangelism.

3. General Revelation and Redemptive Analogies

As was discussed in the previous chapter, two mistakes can be made about general revelation; too little can be expected from general revelation and also too much can be expected from it. Though God has revealed himself in creation and in the conscience of man, the extent of this general revelation is limited. There is a danger of equating general revelation with the means of salvation, the salvific information, that can only be transmitted to us through special revelation.

One popular means of contextualizing Christian faith has been redemptive analogies. Redemptive analogies seek in a target culture some analogy of salvation that can be used for evangelism and in several cases has been beneficial. However determining whether the source of redemptive analogy is actually the human culture itself or indeed a general revelation about God becomes problematic. Chua affirms that, "the concept of the redemptive analogy is not an unproblematic one, for it begs the question regarding the theological validity of implanted divine revelation in any language, or culture" (Chua 2006, 238). In short, are cultural elements planted by God in their culture or are they simply the invention of human culture? If we are counting on a particular redemptive analogy being from general revelation and they actually come from human culture, we may be setting people up for syncretism and compromise. The limitations and qualifications of general revelation remain (Demarest 1989), but as "a rule of thumb, evangelicals are more willing to look positively on contextual models in which general revelation in the context *illuminates*, *illustrates*, or *enhances* our understanding of special revelation" (Moreau 2012, 67). Though we believe that God uses general revelation, we must not lose sight that the clear message of the gospel is most clearly and ultimately found in special revelation.

How, then, can they call on the one they have not believed in? And how can they believe in the one of whom they have not heard? And how can they hear without someone preaching to them? (Rom 10:14).

4. Issues Related to Spiritual Warfare

One of the key reasons Japan is an unreached people group is due to real challenges of spiritual resistance and warfare (Mehn 2017, 17-24). The spiritual history of Japan portrays that the country is bound by evil spiritual forces. This spiritual warfare has been cited as one of the main reasons for missionary attrition in Japan.

Along with enemies of the flesh and the world, we want to affirm that Christ has conquered the powers and authorities (Col 2:10) and we are not aware of the schemes of the evil one (2 Cor 2:11). The Christian is protected by a powerful One as the Apostle John attests, "Greater is He who is in you than he was in the world" (1 John 4:4). Christ has obtained the victory for us, "having disarmed the powers and authorities, he made a public spectacle of them, triumphing over them by the cross" (Col 2:15).

Some Christians while reflecting on Japanese religious beliefs may be tempted to equate the beings from the Japanese unseen spiritual world, such as *goryō, oni, or moenbokoke,* as a manifestation of what the Bible calls demons. While sinister spiritual forces are constantly at work deceiving us and working to generate fear (cf. 2 Cor 4:3-4, 1 Tim 4:1), it would be difficult to identify every instance of these Japanese beliefs by paralleling them with biblical demons or "unclean spirits."

Some others may also view these spirit beings believed by the Japanese as what is referred to by some Christian teachers as "territorial spirits." The problem in equating these territorial spirits with Japanese local gods is a worldview problem. Those that purport that territorial spirits exist seem to have a worldview that is more likely as animistic as the Japanese (Mehn 2017, 19). Hiebert warns that in our effort to include these concerns we could also return to a Christianized version of animism (Hiebert 1994, 200).

Conclusion

To sow the gospel in Japanese soil we have considered several concerns for Christian advance in Japan including several ministry applications for people working on the frontlines of Japanese soil. We must be serious about Japanese religious beliefs and engage the culture through contact points, research, determining needs and providing Christian answers. We have also considered developing theology in seven distinctive areas and we considered four further areas that need to maintain theological balance.

Before we end this book, the next chapter will outline a few very practical principles and practices of sowing and harvesting in the Japanese soil.

9

Sowing and Harvesting Practices

My wife has a Bible study made up of predominately non-believers. One day she asked these ladies why they continued to come to study the Bible. One quickly reacted, "I am finally finding answers to the struggles in my life." The others spoke up as well by reinforcing that their lives were impacted in very deep and practical ways though the scriptures.

We affirm that the gospel is the answer to all social and personal problems. The good news of the gospel announces that we have been rescued and freed and that Jesus has done all that is necessary for us to be reconciled to God and enjoy him and his blessings. The reception of this truth transforms us and those around us. And we know that sowing the gospel in Japanese soil will result in a harvest of much fruit.

Faced with the nature of religion in Japan there are some concrete practices for us who are on the frontlines working with Japanese. These principles are the priority of prayer, proclaiming the gospel, and working for the renewal of the Japanese church.

Pray and Mobilize Prayer

Pray for yourself in the midst of battle. We are in the midst of spiritual warfare where Satan is blinding the eyes of unbelievers (2 Cor 4:4). Pray for your spiritual protection from the enemies of the flesh, the world, and the devil. We need to pray for wisdom and for God to open our eyes like Elisha's servant (2 Kgs 6:17) to see spiritual answers for the Japanese. Pray for courage to do what is radically necessary in your own spiritual life and in your ministry.

Pray for the Japanese who need God, intercede for them to your heavenly Father. Ask God to remove the scales from their eyes, for the Holy Spirit to convict them, for their repentance, and for their faith in Jesus as their Savior. Besides their spiritual needs, pray for those suffering around you, for those with health issues, inner struggles, and those who need direction. Tell them you pray for them. Pray with them in person if appropriate.

Pray for a spiritual breakthrough in Japan. Without a breakthrough from God these major barriers to faith in Japan will not be broken. "The major commitment must be to intercession so that every barrier - whether moral, political or spiritual - be broken down and the Kingdom of the Lord Jesus Christ come" (Johnstone 1995, 161). Besides yourself mobilize many others to pray for you and your specific ministry and to also pray for this breakthrough in Japan.

Prayer is an essential spiritual resource and we should all pray fervently that God will supernaturally work in our lives and in the lives of the Japanese.

Effectively Proclaim the Gospel

There is no room to include here a comprehensive survey on how to best evangelize the Japanese. That task is beyond the scope of this book, although there is room for a few helpful principles.

Sow the Gospel

Sowing the gospel with Japanese is very personal. Get to know Japanese on a personal level. One key to being personal is sharing your own personal story of how you came to faith in Christ. An extremely helpful tool is to write your personal story addressing a Japanese audience about what you were like before, during, and after you trusted Christ as your Savior. Share your story in print and in person.

Evangelizing Japanese is very relational. Aim for developing long-term relationships with Japanese. Use these natural friendships as places for meaningful dialog about your life and faith as well as their lives and their religious beliefs. Seek to win whole families or groups of Japanese to believe in Christ. Evangelism can move quickly through Japanese relational networks.

Proclaiming the gospel among Japanese is a process, often taking some time. Many Japanese are completely unaware of Christ and Bible truths. While being winsome and attractive, patiently pray and guide them toward faith in Christ.

The Gospel and the Japanese

The gospel is relevant to the Japanese as the gospel is relevant to all people's in all places in all times. The redemptive plan of God is so complete that it addresses all the needs of man. The good news of Jesus Christ is the answer to man's social and personal problems. We all need to discover more the depths and riches of the gospel.

The spiritual longings that Japanese religious beliefs reflect can be answered even more satisfactorily through the gospel of Jesus Christ. The true gospel of Christ brings real meaning to our hearts. The task of the church and the missionary is to bring the truth of the gospel - all that Jesus Christ has done for us - to Japanese hearers. Gospel sharing therefore brings biblical meaning and purpose to the questions raised by various Japanese beliefs.

The Japanese culture so often crushes the hearts and spirits of so many individuals in Japan. The gospel has many answers for the Japanese. God in Christ has given us a unique calling and he guides our lives. We are chosen by God (Eph 1:4) and that choosing attaches to us a new identity. Our key identity is wrapped up in God, and not our family, school, work, or group. As shared earlier, we have a God who intimately cares about us and will clearly guide us (Ps 32:8).

Because of Christ we have complete acceptance with God (Rom 17:7). Complete acceptance is great news for Japanese. God's *agape* love is unconditional as we are adopted as his children with true intimacy with the Father God. Assurance of this love drives out any fear (1 John 4:18) whether the source is social pressure or spiritual oppression. The ultimate value for Japanese is not their achievement or their production but the unconditional love of their Heavenly Father. We do not have to be perfect and struggle with perfectionism because Christ was perfect and extends his rightness through justification to us (1 Cor 1:10). Good news for the Japanese is that in Christ we are completely safe in the immanent presence of God and there is no fear of being out of place.

The good news of the gospel is that through Christ we have a Heavenly Father who is almighty and powerful. Because God rules and controls the universe, we do not have to fear our life is random fate without choices. God gives us his strength in regenerating us to become Christians, giving us power in our lives, and transforming us. Change is always possible giving us real hope for Japanese. Because through Christ we can rest from effort and striving, we can have a life of contentment in God's rest (Heb 13:5). Through Christ's redemption, there are no obligations and we are free from enslavement to anything. We are only totally dependent on God as the sovereign provider. There is no shame, no sin, or uncleanliness because of Jesus. Our forgiveness is complete both from guilt and shame.

We can point to the biblical God as the ultimate source of peace and security. How has our experience with God in suffering practically and specifically brought us peace and security? Through the gospel how can the church become a safe place for all?

Proclaim the Gospel

As we are asking people to repent and place their faith in Jesus (1 Thess 1:9) we must have great concern for the belief system of Japanese. We must show them how belief in Jesus can bring greater meaning to their lives, families, and

170

society than their idols and distractions. As outlined by Paul, in Romans 1:18-32, man's search for meaning in the wrong places leads away from glorifying God to idolatry.

Paul on his missionary journeys used proclamation as a means of addressing the belief systems that he encountered. We need to develop responses and apologetics for addressing Japanese beliefs in a systematic manner (see Netland 1985). In order to be prepared to respond as some of the Old Testament prophets like Elijah, Elisha, Isaiah, and Hosea, it would be wise to prepare for questions and explanations related to Japanese beliefs.

The scriptures teach us to minister in Word and deed. Often practical ways gain a hearing for the gospel and reveal us as people who are trustworthy followers of Jesus. This was the case countless times after the Tohoku disaster, as practical help led to relationships with Christians and subsequently sharing of Christ. We must remember to not end with good deeds alone but alongside them to faithfully proclaim the gospel.

Use a variety of ways to communicate the gospel to the Japanese. Besides sermons and your personal testimony be creative using all forms available to you even text messaging, internet videos, and social media. Gospel communication includes everything from storytelling to affective preaching (Fukuda 2001, Hiebert 2012).

Find relational ways for Japanese to connect with other believers, experience the spiritual life of a community of faith, and ultimately to believe. Sometimes Japanese come to faith in Christ in that order. They need to have a sense of belonging. Truth is received through first-hand experience rather than some abstract doctrine. Discussions often allow Japanese as a group to work through ideas and beliefs.

Prepare for the Harvest.
Shifting through many current reports from those working with Japanese, it seems wherever Christ is proclaimed people are coming to Christ. In some places in Japan the desire to evangelize appears to have cooled. But where there is passion for sharing the gospel, Japanese are coming to faith. Recently a key Japanese leader told me that over the years the gospel has been sown all over the Japan but now is the time for harvest.

Our understanding of the longings of the human heart such as a desire to connect with the supernatural, overcoming life's fears, obligation, concern for blessings, the need to belong will bear fruit as we address the religious questions and motivations of Japanese with the gospel.

Work for Renewal of the Church
One of the main reasons cited for the lack of growth of Christianity in Japan is the Japanese church itself. Various factors and issues like

disconnection from society and formalism necessitate renewal in the Japanese church. In my previous book I discuss six interrelated directions needed for transformation of the church in the future (Mehn 2017, 25-49).

Many observers of the Japanese church comment that average Japanese with their beliefs will see very little of interest in Christianity as it is normally presented. Christianity is too transcendental for Japanese understanding and Christianity is not practical enough. In terms of the Japanese culture the church rarely appears to be engaged, while its message is frequently irrelevant, and its community seldom transformational.

As believers in Christ, for the sake of the Japanese church, we need to recover the transforming power of the Gospel for our own lives. The Gospel taught and lived out by the apostles in the New Testament resonated in their hearts. Theirs was an experiential religion lived in constant contact with the surrounding cultures. For many New Testament believers they were ministering to people not unlike those with Japanese religious beliefs. These believers were addressing people's felt religious needs with the glories of Christ.

The Gospel was something that was not only converting those who were worshipping idols but also was changing and sanctifying Christians as well (1 Thess 1:4-10). The Book of Acts has been defined as *Acts of the Holy Spirit* as Luke's account of Christ's gospel working itself out in communities of faith - namely the church. The Holy Spirit was very active in guiding the mission of the church, empowering Christians for bold proclamation, and working at ever increasing levels to sanctify believers and the entire church. This was all the supernatural work of God.

For many Japanese believers, and in the West as well, this Gospel understanding is only intellectual and needs to move down to the heart. In Japan, there are constant accusations that the church focuses too much on the academic and mental side of religion. We do not desire a completely subjective experiential religion. However, as James and others teach, just knowing the correct doctrine intellectually is insufficient to the religion that God intends for us.

The church needs to move out of its institutions and into the street where people are. It is in love and service to these people that we need to find answers from scripture for their spiritual wandering. The church must have the answers in a dynamic faith in Christ and His complete sufficiency for us.

There is hope for the church in Japan because Jesus promises to build his church (Matt 16:18). Though not yet widely known, there are Japanese churches that are healthy, growing, and multiplying with a contagious vision and new paradigms. They are mobilizing lay people, expanding relational evangelism, utilizing small groups, and being creative in ministry. These churches are using new effective models to reproduce the church.

And a vision for church multiplication is growing nationally. Beginning in 2014, the Church Multiplication Vision Festa has cultivated an ambitious vision of planting at least 50,000 new churches in Japan! Along with this church goal is the target of 2% of the population being Christian believers (now it is 0.45%). Throughout Japan, new types of churches that are missional are fostering movements of disciples with the aim of multiplying churches. The church in Japan has much hope for the future.

The Greatest of These

When we first came to Japan, we were introduced to several veteran missionaries. Before we met one veteran couple, we were told that the husband was very skillful in Japanese, however the wife was never quite able to fully get the language. As new missionaries not yet speaking Japanese, we could tell that what we were told was probably true, her language ability was limited.

Several months later at their farewell party a complement was given her from a Japanese believer. He declared, "Her Japanese was never that good, but she loved me into the Kingdom of God!" At that party many others affirmed her love for the Japanese people as significant in their progress to faith in Jesus. Her situation reminds me of the priorities of love in ministry.

> If I speak in the tongues of men or of angels, but do not have love, I am only a resounding gong or a clanging cymbal. If I have the gift of prophecy and can fathom all mysteries and all knowledge, and if I have a faith that can move mountains, but do not have love, I am nothing. If I give all I possess to the poor and give over my body to hardship that I may boast, but do not have love, I gain nothing. (1 Cor 13:1-3)

We are called to a faith of love. We are to love God with everything we are and to love our neighbors (Matt 22:37-39). In ministry our number one motivation is love for people. Love is the greatest thing. We can understand the culture of Japan, be brilliant in our insights in contextualization, skillfully apply the Bible, and follow the best ministry practices, but without love we are nothing and we gain nothing.

There will be many people in the Kingdom of God because you have loved them. You are a recipient of the love of God in Christ. You represent the Father's love as you share Christ. This is the means by which Japanese will believe in Christ. Continue to cultivate in your heart the understanding of God's love for you. Japan is challenging and you will at times not have enough love for the Japanese, but Jesus has all the resource of love for any situation. We need to depend on his love for others. "We love because he first loved us" (1 John 4:19).

Conclusion

We must all love, pray, share, and work together to see the gospel effectively proclaimed to all Japanese, and communities of new disciples multiplied throughout Japan. This will take much hard work, but we have this promise,

> My beloved brothers, be steadfast, immovable, always abounding in the work of the Lord, knowing that in the Lord your labor is not in vain (1 Corinthians 15:58 ESV).

Conclusion

10

Supernatural Faith

Masayo-san began going to the weekly worship service of a new church. After attending several weeks she felt uncomfortable about worshipping idols in her home. She realized that worshipping spirits of animals was sin and so she destroyed these idols. She believed in Jesus Christ as the only true God.

That whole process was very supernatural. Why she came to a church plant and kept coming. How God convicted her of the idols in her home. No one told her that worshipping idols was wrong, and no one instructed her to destroy her idols. She just obeyed God and destroyed her idols. And for sure, her conversion was supernatural as well as her decision to be baptized. In a short period of time you, could see the transformation of her life, her beliefs, and her worldview. The whole process was supernatural.

This story of one Japanese reminded me of Paul's ministry to an entire city, Thessalonica, where many converted from idolatry. How they, "turned to God from idols to serve the living and true God, and to wait for his Son from heaven, whom he raised from the dead—Jesus, who rescues us from the coming wrath." (1 Th 1:9-10). Paul describes that supernatural process by God.

> For we know, brothers and sisters loved by God, that he has chosen you, because our gospel came to you not simply with words but also with power, with the Holy Spirit and deep conviction. You know how we lived among you for your sake. You became imitators of us and of the Lord, for you welcomed the message in the midst of severe suffering with the joy given by the Holy Spirit (1 Thess 1:4-6).

Sowing the gospel is a supernatural work. Notice for the Thessalonians, the Word of God came with power, with the Holy Spirit, and with conviction (v. 5). They believed the Word of God and it manifested in having joy in the midst of suffering (v. 6). That was all supernatural.

The seed of the gospel grew in them as a community of believers and the gospel took further root in their lives and their hearts. And so they,

> became a model to all the believers in Macedonia and Achaia. The Lord's message rang out from you not only in Macedonia and Achaia - your faith in God has become known everywhere. Therefore we do not need to say anything about it (1 Thess 1:7-8).

This empowerment for mission beyond their immediate locality and this multiplication of disciples and churches, was also supernatural.

While all these supernatural workings were going on with the Thessalonian believers, Paul and his ministry team were living among them (v. 5b). They were sharing the word of God, the message of the gospel of Jesus Christ. Their ministry in Thessalonica was not easy but lead to social unrest and accusations of being troublemakers (Acts 17:6). Those faithful witnesses needed supernatural resources during the entire visit. But because Paul and his team worked through these difficulties with those resources, the Thessalonians became imitators of both them and the Lord himself (v. 6a).

As believers in Christ, what are our beliefs? Do we believe in *our* supernatural faith? To see our desire fulfilled that Japan would be reached with the gospel, we are completely dependent on the supernatural. "Mission is ultimately a spiritual task that must be empowered with spiritual resources" (Ott & Strauss 2019, 246). Our ministry does not succeed by techniques, skills, or human ideas but only by the supernatural God.

- We are all dependent on the Holy Spirit, the one that convicts of sin, righteousness, and judgment (John 16:8-11). People blinded by Satan (2 Cor 4:4) must have their eye's opened and regeneration occurs only supernaturally (John 3:3, 5-6).

- The Father sent his Son for us that we may live. And the Son has given us the Spirit who will glorify himself (John 16:13-14, cf. 15:26). That Spirit will teach us and remind us of the truth (John 14:26). That supernatural Spirit gives us spiritual gifts, fills us, empowers us for gospel witness (Acts 1:8), promises to remain with us (John 14:16-17) and will intercede for us (Rom 8:26-27).

- We live and minister in the shadow of the cross of Christ. The purpose of the cross was that, "by his death he might break the power of him who holds the power of death - that is, the devil" (Heb 2:14). That is supernatural. What God has done for us in Christ - his completed atonement - is the power for us to grow and serve as believers.

- The Word of God is supernatural, and it will do what it was sent to accomplish (Isa 55:10-11). Because it has supernatural power (Heb 4:12), the Word should be publicly read, taught, and preached (1 Tim 4:13).

- The gospel message that we sow is supernatural. "For I am not ashamed of the gospel, because it is the power of God that brings salvation to everyone who believes: first to the Jew, then to the Gentile" (Rom 1:16). The gospel is powerful because is it supernatural.

And our ultimate goal is a supernatural one. The goal of incarnational ministry is not that people understand the gospel. It is that they respond to God's invitation and are transformed by his power. They become new creatures through Christ and members of a new community, the church (Hiebert & Meneses 1995, 373).

We desire transforming communities of faith that have a Christian Worldview with Christ as the center of their lives. It is these followers of Christ engaged with their culture and connecting with other Japanese that will bring the Kingdom of God to Japan through multiplying churches.

Then what is our role in that big picture? Sowing the gospel in Japanese soil is supernatural. Our role is to live among the Japanese, while we depend on the supernatural resources of the Father's calling and guidance, the Son's cross and his gospel, and the Holy Spirit's gifting and empowerment. We are to be faithful in proclaiming Jesus, warning, and teaching every Japanese, using all the wisdom we receive from God. That Christ may reign in Japanese hearts as devoted worshippers of the living and true God.

> He is the one we proclaim, admonishing and teaching everyone with all wisdom, so that we may present everyone fully mature in Christ. To this end I strenuously contend with all the energy Christ so powerfully works in me (Colossians 1:28-29)

References

Allen, Roland. *Spontaneous Expansion of the Church and the Causes Which Hinder It.* North American ed. Grand Rapids, MI: Eerdmans, 1962.

Ama, Toshimaru. 2004. *Why Do Japanese Consider Themselves Irreligious? Japanese Spirituality: Being Non-religious in a Religious Culture.* Lanham, Maryland: University Press of America.

Andreasen, Esben. 1993. "Japanese Religions: An Introduction." In Ian Reader, Esben Andreasen, Finn Stefansson eds. *Japanese Religions: Past and Present.* 33-44. New York: Routledge.

Antoni, Klaus. 1993. "Yasukuni-Jinja and Folk Religion." In Mark R. Mullins, Shimazono Susumu, Paul L. Swanson eds. *Religion & Society in Modern Japan: Selected Readings.* 121-32. Nagoya, Japan: Nanzan Institute for Religion and Culture.

Ayabe, Henry. 1992. *Step Inside: Japan: Language Culture Mission.* Tokyo: Japan Evangelical Missionary Association.

Basabe, Fernando M. 1972. *Japanese Religious Attitudes.* Maryknoll, NY: Orbis Books.

Befu, Harumi. 1971. *Japan: An Anthropology Introduction.* San Francisco: Chandler Publishing Co.

Benedict, Ruth. 1946. *The Chrysanthemum and the Sword: Patterns of Japanese Culture.* New York: Times Mirror.

Bennett, Robert H. 2013. "Islands of the Gods: Productive and Unproductive Missionary Methods in Animistic Societies -Roland Allen's Examination of Saint Paul's Use of Miracles." In Craig Ott and J. D. Payne Eds. *Missionary Methods: Research, Reflections, and Realities.* 145–156. Pasadena, CA: William Carey Library.

Berentsen, Jan-Martin. 1985 "Ancestor Worship in Missiological Perspective." In Bong Rin Ro ed. *Christian Alternatives to Ancestor Practices.* 261-85. Taichung, Taiwan: Asia Theological Association.

Braun, Neil. 1971. *Laity Mobilized: Reflections on Church Growth in Japan and Other Lands.* Grand Rapids, MI: Wm. B. Eerdmans Publishing Co.

Chizuo, Shibata. 1985. "Some Problematic Aspects of Japanese Ancestor Worship." In Bong Rin Ro ed. *Christian Alternatives to Ancestor Practices.* 247- 60. Taichung, Taiwan: Asia Theological Association.

Chua, How Chuang. 2006. "Revelation in the Chinese Characters: Divine or Divined?" In Gailyn Van Rheenen. *Contextualization and Syncretism: Navigating Cultural Currents.* EMS 13 229-42. Pasadena, CA: William Carey

Library.

Clark, Paul. 1986. "Understanding the Resistance of Japan to Christianity." *Japan Harvest.* Vol. 36, No. 2, 1986. 26-29.

_____. 1987. "The Gospel in the Context of the Japanese Worldview." In *The Gospel Encounters the Japanese Worldview: Bridges or Barriers.* Fritz Sprunger ed. 24-28. 1987 Hayama Missionary Seminar.

Conn, Harvey. 1984. *Eternal Word and Changing Worlds.* Phillipsburg, NJ: P & R Publishing.

Conrad, Stan. 1997. "Encountering Japanese Resistance." In J. Dudley Woodberry ed. *Reaching the Resistant: Barriers and Bridges for Mission.* EMS 6. 117-31. Pasadena, CA: William Carey Library.

Corwin, Charles. 1962. "The Japanese Concept of God." *Japan Harvest.* Spring 1962. 18-20.

_____.1972. *East to Eden: Religion and the Dynamics of Social Change.* Grand Rapids, MI: Wm. B. Eerdmans Publishing Co.

_____. 1978. "Japanese Bonsai or/and California Redwood." *Missiology: An International Review* 6 (3): 297-310.

Dale, Kenneth J. 1975. *Circle of Harmony: A Case Study in Popular Buddhism with Implications for Christian Mission.* Pasadena, CA: William Carey Library.

_____. 1995. *Coping with Culture: The Current Struggle of the Japanese Church.* Tokyo:

Lutheran Booklet Press.

_____. 1998. "Why the Slow Growth of the Japanese Church?" *Missiology: An International Review.* July 1998. 275-88.

Davies, Roger J. 2016. *Japanese Culture: The Religious and Philosophical Foundations.* Tokyo: Tuttle Publishing.

Davis, Winston. 1992. *Japanese Religion and Society: Paradigms of Structure and Change.* New York: State University of New York Press.

Dore, R. P. 1958. *City Life in Japan: A Study of a Tokyo Ward.* Berkeley, CA: Univ. of California Press.

Dyer, Stanley R. 2013. *Communication in Community.* Bellville, ON: Guardian Books.

Earhart, H. Byron. 1969. *Japanese Religion: Unity and Diversity.* Belmont, CA: Dickenson Publishing Co. Inc.

_____. 2004. *Japanese Religion: Unity and Diversity.* Fourth Edition. Boston, MA: Wadsworth.

_____. 2014. *Religion in Japan: Unity and Diversity.* Fifth Edition. Boston, MA: Wadsworth.

Ellwood, Robert. 2008. *Introducing Japanese Religion.* New York, NY: Routledge.

Erickson J. Millard. 1985. *Christian Theology.* Grand Rapids, MI: Baker Book House.

Flemming, Dean. 2005. *Contextualizing in the New Testament: Patterns for Theology and Mission.*

Downers Grove, IL: IVP Academic.

Fujisawa, Chikao. 1958. *Concrete Universality of the Japanese Way of Thinking: A New Interpretation of Shintoism.* Tokyo: Hokuseido Press.

Fukuda, Mitsuo. 1993. *Developing a Contextualized Church: As a Bridge to Christianity in Japan.* Gloucester, UK: Wide Margin Books.

_____. 2001. "Sermon Topics Contextualized for Japan." *Journal of Asian Mission* 3 (1): 141–48.

_____. 2015. "Toward a New Breed of Churches in Japan." In *Becoming the People of God: Creating Christ-centered Communities in Buddhist Asia*, edited by Paul H. de Neui. Seanet Volume 11. 21-30. Pasadena, CA: William Carey Library.

Furuya, Yasuo. ed. trans. 1997. *A History of Japanese Theology.* Grand Rapids, MI: Eerdmans.

_____. 2006. *History of Japan and Christianity.* Ageo-shi, Saitama Seigakuin University Press.

Garon, Sheldon M. 1986. "State and Religion in Imperial Japan, 1912-1945." *Journal of Japanese Studies* 12 (2): 273-302.

Hardacre, Helen. 1986. Kurozumikyo and the New Religions of Japan. Princeton, NJ: Princeton University Press.

Heisswolf, Martin. 2018. *Japanese Understanding*

of Salvation: Soteriology in the Context of Japanese Animism. Carlisle, Cumbria: UK. Langham Global Library.

Hesselgrave, David J. "Syncretism: Mission and Missionary Induced?" In Gailyn Van Rheenen. *Contextualization and Syncretism*: Navigating Cultural Currents. EMS 13 71-98. Pasadena, CA: William Carey Library.

Hesselgrave, David J. and Edward Rommen. 2000. *Contextualization: Meanings, Methods, and Models*. Pasadena, CA: William Carey Library.

Hiebert, Laurence D. 2012. "Employing Varied Japanese Cultural Forms to Illustrate Biblical Truths." D.Min. major project, Trinity International University.

Hiebert, Paul G. 1982. "The Flaw of the Excluded Middle." *Missiology: An International Review*. January 1982. 35-47.

_____. 1999. "The Flaw of the Excluded Middle." In Ralph D. Winter and Steven C. Hawthorne. *Perspectives on the World Christian Movement: A Reader*. 3rd ed. 414-21. Pasadena, CA: William Carey Library.

_____. 1984a. *Anthropological Insights for Missionaries*. Grand Rapids, MI: Baker Book House.

_____. 1984b. "Critical Contextualization." *Missiology: An International Review* 12 (3): 287-96.

_____.1994. *Anthropological Reflections on*

Missiological Issues. Grand Rapids, MI: Baker Book House.

Hiebert, Paul G. and Eloise Hiebert Meneses. 1995. *Incarnational Ministry: Planting Churches in Band, Tribal, Peasant, and Urban Societies.* Grand Rapids, MI: Baker Book House.

Hiebert, Paul G., R. Daniel Shaw and Tite Tienou. 1999. *Understanding Folk Religion: A Christian Response to Popular Beliefs and Practices.* Grand Rapids, MI: Baker Book House.

Hori, Ichiro. 1967. "Appearance of Individual Self-consciousness in Japanese Religion and Its Historical Transformations." In *The Japanese Mind: Essentials of Japanese Philosophy and Culture.* Charles Moore ed. 201-27. Honolulu: East West Center Press.

_____.1968. *Folk Religion in Japan: Continuity and Change.* Chicago: Univ. of Chicago Press.

_____. ed. 1972. *Japanese Religion: A Survey by the Agency for Cultural Affairs.* Tokyo: Kodansha International Ltd.

Iglehart, Charles W. 1957. *Cross and Crisis in Japan.* New York: Friendship Press.

Jennings, J. Nelson. 2003. "Theology in Japan." In Handbook on Christianity in Japan. *Handbook of Oriental Studies, Section Five, Japan,* ed. Mark R. Mullins, 181–203. Boston: Brill.

Johnstone, Patrick. 1995. "Biblical Intercession: Spiritual Power to Change our World." In *Spiritual Power and Missions: Raising the Issues*

Edited by Edward Rommen, EMS 3 137-65.
Pasadena, CA: William Carey Library.

Keller, Timothy J. 2012. *Center Church*. Grand
Rapids, MI: Zondervan.

Kodansha. 1993. *Japan: An Illustrated
Encyclopedia*. Tokyo: Kodansha.

Kwast, L. E. 1992. "Understanding Culture." In R.
D. Winter and S. C. Hawthorne Ed. *Perspectives
on the World Christian Movement*: A Reader
Rev. ed. C3-C6. Pasadena, CA: William Carey
Library.

Lausanne Covenant. 1974.
www.lausanne.org/content/covenant/lausan
ne-covenant.

Lebra, Takie Sugiyama. 1976. *Japanese Patterns of
Behavior*. Honolulu: University of Hawaii
Press.

Lee, Robert. 1967. *Stranger in the Land: A Study of
the Church in Japan*. World Studies of
Churches in Mission. London: Lutterworth
Press.

_____, ed. 1995. *The Japanese Emperor
System: The Inescapable Missiological Issue*.
Tokyo: Tokyo Mission Research Institute.

_____. 1999. *The Clash of Civilizations: An
Intrusive Gospel in Japanese Civilization*.
Harrisburg, PA: Trinity Press International.

Lewis, David C. 1993. *The Unseen Face of Japan*.
Tunbridge Wells, UK: Monarch Publications.

_____. 2001. "Questioning Assumptions

About Japanese Society." In Cynthia Dufty ed. *The Unseen Face of Japan: Culturally Appropriate Communication of the Gospel.* 11-29. 2001 Hayama Missionary Seminar.

_____. 2013. *The Unseen Face of Japan.* 2nd Edition. Gloucester, UK: Wide Margin.

_____. 2018. *Religion in Japanese Daily Life.* New York: Routledge.

Luke, Percy T. 1970. "Japanese Concepts of Death." In Arthur Reynolds ed. *Japan in Review: Japan Harvest Anthology.* 64-65. Japan Evangelical Missionary Association.

Lundell, Peter N. 1995. "Behind Japan's Resistant Web: Understanding the Problem of Nihonkyo." *Missiology: An International Review.* October 1995. 401-12.

Matheisen, Gaylan Kent. 2006. *A Theology of Mission: Challenges and Opportunities in Northeast Asia.* Minneapolis, MN: Lutheran University Press.

McFarland, H. Neill. 1967. *The Rush Hour of the Gods: A Study in New Religious Movements in Japan.* New York: Macmillan Co.

McGavran, Donald. 1985. "Honoring Ancestors in Japan." In Bong Rin Ro ed. *Christian Alternatives to Ancestor Practices.* 303-18. Taichung, Taiwan: Asia Theological Association.

Meeko, A. Leon. 2001 "Fluid Opportunity – Ministry in 'Post-modern' Japan." *Japan*

Mission Journal. 2001 Autumn. 184-190.

Mehn, John Wm. 2017. *Multiplying Churches in Japanese Soil.* Pasadena, CA: William Carey Library.

Milhous, Ken. 1984. "Japanese Christians and the Departed." Unpublished paper.

Miyazaki, Kentaro. 2003. "The Kakure Kirishitan Tradition." In *Handbook on Christianity in Japan. Handbook of Oriental Studies, Section Five, Japan*, ed. Mark R. Mullins, 19–34. Boston: Brill.

Moreau, A. Scott. 2005. "Contextualization." In *The Changing Face of World Missions*, by Michael Pocock, Gailyn Van Rheenen and Douglas McConnell, 321–48. Grand Rapids, MI: Baker Academic.

_____. 2012. *Contextualization in World Missions: Mapping and Assessing Evangelical Models.* Grand Rapids, MI: Kregel Academic.

_____. 2018. *Contextualizing the Faith: A Holistic Approach.* Grand Rapids, MI: Baker Academic.

Mullins, Mark R. 1998. *Christianity Made in Japan: A Study of Indigenous Movements.* Honolulu: University of Hawaii Press.

_____. 2006. "Japanese Christianity." In *Nanzan Guide to Japanese Religions,* eds. Paul Loren Swanson and Clark Chilson. Honolulu, HI: 115–28. University of Hawaii Press.

_____. 2012. "Secularization,

Deprivatization, and the Reappearance of 'Public Religion' in Japanese Society." *Journal of Religion in Japan*. 1 (2012) 61-82.

Mullins, Mark R., Shimazono Susumu and Paul L. Swanson eds. 1993. *Religion & Society in Modern Japan*. Tokyo: Asian Humanities Press.

Nakamaki, Hirochika. 2003. *Japanese Religions at Home and Abroad: Anthropological Perspectives*. New York: Routledge.

Nakane, Chie. 1970.. *Japanese Society*. Tokyo: Charles E. Tuttle Company.

Netland, Harold A. 1985. "Apologetics and Contemporary Japanese Worldview." *Japan Harvest*. No. 4 1985/86. 6-8.

_____. 1991. *Dissonant Voices: Religious Pluralism and the Question of Truth*. Grand Rapids, MI: William B. Eerdmans Publishing Co.

_____. 2015. *Christianity & Religious Diversity: Clarifying Christian Commitments in a Globalizing Age*. Grand Rapids, MI: Baker Academic.

Ott, Craig. 2015. "Globalization and Contextualization: Reframing the Task of Contextualization in the Twenty-first Century." *Missiology: An International Review* 43 (1): 43–58.

Ott, Craig and Steven J. Strauss. 2010. *Encountering Theology of Mission: Biblical Foundations, Historical Development, and*

Contemporary Issues. Grand Rapids, MI: Baker Academic.

Ott, Craig and Gene Wilson. 2011. *Global Church Planting: Biblical Principles and Best Practices for Multiplication.* Grand Rapids, MI: Baker Academic.

Ono, Sokyo. 1962. *Shinto: The Kami Way.* Tokyo: Charles E. Tuttle: Tokyo.

Prohl, Inken. 2012. "New Religions in Japan: Adaptations and Transformations in Contemporary Society." In *The Handbook of Contemporary Japanese Religion,* edited by Inken Prohl and John K. Nelson, 241–67. Lieden, Nederlands: Brill

Plath, David. 1964. "Where the Family of God is the Family: The Role of the Dead in Japanese Households" *American Anthropologist,* Vol.66, 300–317.

Reader, Ian. 1991. *Religion in Contemporary Japan.* Honolulu: University of Hawaii Press.

Reader, Ian and George J. Tanabe Jr. 1998. *Practically Religious: Worldly Benefits and the Common Religion of Japan.* Honolulu: University of Hawaii Press.

Ro, Bong Rin ed. 1985. *Christian Alternatives to Ancestor Practices.* Taichung, Taiwan: Asia Theological Association.

Ronan, David W. 1999. "Conversion, Lordship, and Mission: Contextualizing Theology in Light of Japanese Ancestral Practices." Unpublished paper.

Ross, John B. ed. 1980. *Man's Religions* 6th ed. New York: Macmillan Publishing Co, Inc.

Shenk, Wilbert R. 2016. "Christians, Social Location, and Religious Plurality." In Wilbert R. Shenk and Richard J. Plantinga eds. *Christianity and Religious Plurality: Historical and Global Perspectives.* 49–70. Eugene, OR: Wipf & Stock Publishers.

Shimazono, Susumu. 2003. "New Religions and Christianity." In *Handbook on Christianity in Japan.* Handbook of Oriental Studies, Section Five, Japan, edited by Mark R. Mullins. 277-94. Boston: Brill.

Smart, Ninian. 1969. *The Religious Experience of Mankind.* New York: Charles Scribner's and Sons.

Smith, Robert J. 1974. *Ancestor Worship in Contemporary Japan.* Stanford, CA: Stanford University Press.

Solheim, Dagfinn. 1984. "Japanese Culture and the Christian Church." *Missiology: An International Review.* Vol XII, No. 2. April 1984. 213-21.

Spae, Joseph J. 1968. *Christianity Encounters Japan.* Tokyo: Oriens Institute for Religious Research.

Stark, Rodney. 1999. "Secularization, R.I.P." in *Sociology of Religion.* Volume 60, Issue 3. 1 October 1999, 249–273.

Steyne, Philip. 1989. *Gods of Power: A Study of the Beliefs and Practices of Animists.* Dallas: Touch

Outreach Ministries.

Sugimoto, Yoshio. 2014. *An Introduction to Japanese Society.* 4th ed. Cambridge University Press.

Swyngedouw, Jan. 1993. "Religion in Contemporary Japanese Society." In Mark R. Mullins, Shimazono Susumu, Paul L. Swanson eds. *Religion & Society in Modern Japan: Selected Readings.* 49-72. Nagoya, Japan: Nanzan Institute for Religion and Culture.

Taylor, Jared. 1983. *Shadows of the Rising Sun: A Critical View of the "Japanese Miracle."* NY: Quill.

Ueda, Kenji. 1972. "Shinto." In Ichiro Hori, ed. *Japanese Religion: A Survey by the Agency for Cultural Affairs.* 29-45. Tokyo: Kodansha International.

Uemura, Toshifumi. 2001. "The Way to State Shinto In Comparison with Shrine Shinto." In Cynthia Dufty ed. *The Unseen Face of Japan: Culturally Appropriate Communication of the Gospel.* 5-9. 2001 Hayama Missionary Seminar.

Uenuma, Masao. 1988. "Christian Spirituality in Buddhist Context." In Fritz Sprunger ed. *Incarnating the Gospel in the Japanese Context.* 14-36. 1988 Hayama Missionary Seminar.

Van Rheenen, Gailyn. 1991. *Communicating Christ in Animistic Contexts.* Pasadena, CA: William Carey Library.

_____. *Contextualization and Syncretism: Navigating Cultural Currents.* EMS 13. Pasadena, CA: William Carey Library.

Winter, Ralph D. 2002. "From Mission to Evangelism to Mission." *International Journal of Frontier Missiology.* 19 (4): 6–8.

Yamaguchi, Noboru. 1985. "What Does the New Testament Say about Ancestor Practices." In Bong Rin Ro ed. *Christian Alternatives to Ancestor Practices.* 43-54. Taichung, Taiwan: Asia Theological Association.

Index

Z

Dedication

This book is dedicated to everyone who has sown the gospel among the Japanese.

Acknowledgements

This book is a product of years of work and would not have happened without the encouragement and assistance of several important people. The late Dr. Paul Hiebert encouraged my work along these lines and inspired me to write, especially for the Japanese context. Dr. David Lewis was very helpful with his scholarship, friendship, and practical help. Dr. Gary Fujino was enthusiastic for the project spanning many years and his practical advice regarding the content was extremely helpful. Dr. Rick Shenk and Dr. Nobuo Watanabe reviewed drafts of parts of this book with their expertise in theology, missiology, and the Japanese culture. Baker Book House generously extended their permission to use the key diagrams in this book. My dear wife Elaine who was a constant encouragement, supportive advisor, and tireless proofreader of the manuscript. And many missionaries and Japanese discussed with me their understanding of this topic, their struggles, possible solutions, and hopes.

About the Author

John Wm. Mehn and his wife Elaine have served as Converge Worldwide (formerly Baptist General Conference) missionaries in Japan since 1985. John's primary ministries have included cross-cultural church planting, leadership development, equipping for church planting, and spiritual renewal mentoring. John has a Doctorate of Ministry in Missiology from Trinity International University.

Other Books by this Author

Thank you for purchasing *Sowing the Gospel in Japanese Soil: Understanding Japanese Religious Beliefs* by John Wm. Mehn.

His previous book was *Multiplying Churches in Japanese Soil* published in 2017 by William Carey Library was well received. It is available in paperback or Ebook from the publisher and also on Amazon.

Other Books Available from Gospel Rest Resources

Elaine Mehn completed her first devotional book *Thoughts Along the Way* in 2002, a collection of 52 weekly devotions indexed by Scripture and Topic. Find it on Amazon.

Coming soon – *Thoughts Along the Way* in Japanese.

In 2018, Elaine completed her follow up devotional book *More Thoughts Along the Way: Grace-based Devotions for Spiritual Nourishment.* Find it on Amazon.

If you would like to purchase any book directly from GospelRest Resources, please write us at info@GospelRest.com. Or visit our website at https://www.gospelrest.com/our-books/.

Just Released

Grace for Everyday: A Group Study for Spiritual Growth. This is the English version of a group discussion–based Bible study written to encourage spiritual growth. A separate Japanese volume of these studies will be available soon.

Made in the USA
Monee, IL
17 April 2024

56836749R00118